Scandalous Love

A Novel

By

Qiana London

ISBN: 1-4107-5564-9 (e-book)
ISBN: 1-4107-5563-0 (Paperback)

This book is printed on acid free paper.

1stBooks – rev. 05/13/03

Author's Note

During the past year and a half a lot happened which opened my eyes and matured me quick, fast, and in a hurry. These trials and tribulations allowed me time to self-reflect. I reevaluated my character and purpose. I now realize at times it's hard to see a situation for what it is when one is actually involved. Once a person is removed, though, all aspects can be viewed for what they really are. I'm thankful for each experience. Each one allowed me to learn and grow. Fortunately, I can recognize that now. While going through, my reaction wasn't always so civil but prayer and guidance got me through. Taking heed to my grandfather's advice "don't get mad, get smart", I placed my energy into something more productive... this novel... and it is only the beginning. I realize the hardships are not over... but guess what – I'm ready.

Acknowledgements

First and foremost, I have to give praise and honor to the **One** who blessed me with the gift of writing... **Lord**, I know you didn't bring me this far to leave me behind now – **Your Will** be done! I cannot thank You enough.

Next, **Mama**: Thank you for staying in my corner and supporting me through every project I have ever worked on – I get my drive from you! **Renay Jackson**: Words cannot express my appreciation for you. Timing is everything and you could not have come into my life at a better time. Thank you for believing in me and sharing your knowledge. Let's do our thing – write on! **Phat Efx**: Dre, thanks for your words of encouragement. Gabriel, you represented once again! You guys definitely do your thing and I am forever grateful. **God Mommy**: For the countless hours spent at your house on your computer. **Sister**: For continuously having my back... you fuss but you always come through. **Cuddy**: For putting me in touch with

Renay and for your continuous motivation – you never doubted I could do it. My cousin, **Mistah F.A.B**: Our conversations are never held in vain. You have a way of communicating. You always tell me what I need to know, not necessarily what I want to hear and I love you for that. You and your words motivate me more than you'll ever know. I love you. **To all of my family and friends** who've supported me in more ways than one... much love forever!

Chapter One

My ear was warm and sweaty from holding the phone for two hours. Zereck was on the opposite end of my line apologizing for missing our dinner dates two nights in a row. He continued to talk but all I heard were sounds in my ear as my mind drifted. He hadn't been so thoughtless in the beginning of our, now, two year relationship. My instincts were telling me there was another woman but my pride said otherwise. Besides, I'd given him several opportunities to tell me the truth and for what it was worth I chose to believe him.

"Baby, are you listening to me?"

"I heard you Zereck. So you're leaving for Los Angeles in three hours, huh?"

"Yeah, our promoter booked us a show."

"Okay Zereck, do what you've got to do."

"That's it?"

"There is nothing else to say, Z. This is what you've been talking about since high school."

"Then why do I get the feeling you're not happy for me?"

"Of course I'm happy for you, Zereck. I'm not happy for us. You are always putting everything else before me. There was a time when I was first and then there was the rest of the world."

"Dezzy, you know you are my world but I have to take advantage of this opportunity."

"Look, I'm sorry, Z. I'm being selfish and that's not right. I hardly get to see you any more and when we do it's for a hot second. I miss you."

"I won't be gone long. I'll call you as soon as I get there okay?"

"You better and be careful."

When I hung up the phone I was pissed. I'll admit it. Our relationship was getting old fast. I was trying to hang in there because Zereck was my first love, my high school sweetheart. As time went on we were growing farther apart. The urge to move on was there but so was the belief he would come around and we would go back to the way we were.

2

I turned the key and my engine roared. I always got in my car and drove around when I wanted to clear my head. I didn't have a specific destination and it didn't matter. I wanted to get away and have time to myself. I flipped through the radio stations trying to find a song that suited my mood. Unsuccessful, I put in my Toni Braxton CD and bypassed all of the songs until I reached "Just Be a Man About It".

I had been driving for over an hour and ended up in Milpitas at The Great Mall. It had been a while since I'd gone hat shopping and there was no time like the present. Like always, I entered the mall with one thing in mind but ended up buying much more than I should have. It was all right, I would raise my prices this week on my clients. I'd make the money back in no time. The smell of Wilson's Leather called me right into the store. I had no willpower.

"Is there anything I can help you with today?" The salesclerk was an energetic blonde. She hadn't let me get three feet in the door.

"I'm just looking, thanks."

"Dezzy, you don't remember me do you?"

"I'm sorry, should I?" I tried my best not to sound rude.

"We went to the same high school. We were physical education buddies in Block C, remember?"

"Cindy?"

"Yes! What are you doing these days?"

"I'm a beautician and make-up artist, you?"

"Well, I'm home for the summer. I'll begin working on my Masters at Stanford in the fall."

"Oh, that's nice!" I wanted to get as far away from her as I could.

"Are you still writing?"

"Whenever I get a free moment."

"That's great! You've always had a way with words."

"Thanks, that means a lot to me."

"Is there anything in particular you're looking for?"

"I want a leather hat."

"They're right this way."

I allowed Cindy to be helpful then got as far away from the store as possible. I was not in a sociable mood. I was getting an Oatmeal-Raisin cookie from Mrs. Fields when my cell phone rang.

"What up, ugly?" she said
"Hey, Lee."
"Damn, why do you sound like you lost your puppy?"
"I don't want to talk about it."
"Girl, you know you can't keep anything from me."

My God Sister was right. I told her everything and even if I tried to hide it she always managed to find out. She was the one I always turned to when I was having male problems. Naturally, I pulled up in front of her house later that evening.

"What did his ass do now, D?"
"It's what he doesn't do. I barely see him anymore."
"Shit, count your blessings."
"I'm serious, Lee. One mind tells me to drop his ass and the other says I should stick it out."
"D, I think better on a full stomach. Have you eaten?"
"Not really, I haven't had much of an appetite."
"Well, you better develop one by the time we reach Black Angus."

I was picking at my baked potato as Lee polished off her second margarita. I thought spending time with my God Sister would help keep my mind off Zereck but it only made matters worse.

"Dezzy, you're life didn't begin with Zereck and it won't end with him either."

"You're right. I wish I'd started seeing different people when the red flags started going up."

"It's never too late to start."

"I sometimes wonder if he's seeing another woman."

"He'd have to be a fool to let someone like you go."

"Yeah, you would think so but you can't give a man too much credit. I've had to learn the hard way."

"Dezzy, you've been putting more energy into the relationship than it's worth. It's time to move on."

"You're right. How will I know when to do it?"

"Trust your instincts."

"How will I know when it's the right time?"

"Why waste any more time?"

"That's true. As soon as he gets back from Los Angeles, I'm cutting his ass off."

Lee picked up her glass of water but sat it down before the glass ever touched her lips.

"What's wrong, Lee? You look like you saw a ghost."

The waitress walked by our table and Lee pulled her by the arm. From the expression on the woman's face, it was obvious Lee caught her off guard. "Can we have the check, please?"

"Lee, do you want to clue me in on what the hell is going on?"

By now, I turned around to see what had suddenly gained her attention. I didn't realize I'd begin shaking until Lee took the fork out of my hand.

"Dezzy, let's leave. Now isn't the time or the place."

Zereck was being seated in the restaurant with a female. The waiter walked away and he took her hand in his. He had never looked at me the way he was looking at this woman. "You have got to be kidding me," I said.

He was totally consumed by this bright-eyed, bushy-tailed bitch. She wore a long weave and acrylic nails far from believable. Her frame was petite and disproportionate from what I could see, and she hid behind layers of make-up. Hell, who am I kidding? I could talk about this woman until I was blue in the face. Shabba or not, she was here with my man – correction, ex-man.

"Let's go, D."

"No. I'm going to confront him."

"Look, we don't need to make a scene in this restaurant."

"Lee, damn. I'm a grown woman. I know how to act."

I stood up from the table and Lee was on my heels. It seemed I was walking in slow motion towards Zereck's table. My knees felt weak as I became close. I considered turning around when I realized I didn't know what I was going to say. I knew I would kick myself later, though, if I didn't get closure.

"What happened to Los Angeles, Z?" I was calm.

"Dezzy, I... I –"

"You what? You lied to me, Z and you didn't have to. All I asked were you give it to me straight and you couldn't do that! I've been nothing but good to your sorry ass and this is how you repay me? Well, I hope like hell it was worth it, Zereck because I'm tired of this shit. I'm done playing games, I'm done making excuses, and I'm done with you. Do me a favor, forget my number and forget you ever knew me. Goodbye, Zereck." I could feel his eyes on my back but I didn't turn around. I had been so civil the people dining had no clue of what had taken place.

I didn't bother going inside Lee's house when we got back. I didn't want to entertain the events of the evening any longer. I wanted to be in the confinement of my own home where I could sulk alone. When I walked in the door, my brother was in the living room with my mother. I'd moved back home to save up some money. My brother never left. He pulled his weight and helped my mother with the bills, though. He was far from a free-loader. My mother was gone on business majority of the time so we often had the house to ourselves.

"Dezzy, baby, leave your shoes at the door. I shampooed the carpet."

I complied, said brief hellos, and went into my room. I tried to hold back the tears. I held them long enough to get to my room but I had no control over the constant streams running down my cheeks, now. Like a zombie, I aimlessly moved around my room. Three Mary J. Blige CDs later, I laid down on my bed and stared at the ceiling in my t-shirt and panties enjoying the cool breeze coming through my windows. As much as I tried not to, I kept replaying the incident in the restaurant over and over in my head. Of course, I was thinking of everything I should have said but it was too late now. The more I thought about it, the angrier I became. Fortunately, I was able to find solace knowing it was finally over.

Donte knocked on my door three times, our signal knock. I pulled on a pair of shorts then he walked through the door. My brother was my best friend. Our closeness in age made it easier for us to relate to one another. He gulped down a Gatorade and tightened the drawstring on his sweats before falling on the floor into a push-up. I didn't have to tell him when something was bothering me. It was a sixth sense he had. He did thirty push-ups before opening his mouth.

"Damn, Dezzy you need to vacuum. It's a wonder you don't have things growing on your floor."

"I'm always busy Donte and when I get home I'm too tired."

"Whatever. You know, real niggas don't like nasty women."

"Don't start with me, Donte."

"All right, I ain't going to mess with you. What's up?"

"Nothing."

"That bad, huh?"

"Yep."

"Do you want to talk about it?"

"Nope."

"Tomorrow?"

"Maybe."

"I'm off tomorrow so I'm here when you need me."

"Thank you, boo."

"The Simpsons will be on in thirty minutes, you down?"

"Only if we can watch it in here. I'm comfortable."

"That's cool. I'll be back with a sleeping bag and the vacuum cleaner."

Chapter Two

"So the shit hit the fan, huh?"

My eyes hadn't adjusted to the sunlight beaming on my face so I laid there with my eyes closed. I regretted answering the phone now that I heard my cousin in my ear talking about Zereck. However, I knew this wasn't a topic I'd be able to run from forever.

"I see Lee got to you before I did."

"And I'm glad she did. Dezzy, you're better than me. When I got done with Zereck, I wouldn't have been able to show my face in Black Angus again."

"Which is why I'm glad you weren't there."

"Whatever, D. Don't front, are you okay?"

"Camille, I'm not going to lie. I was hurt but I believe everything happens for a reason."

"This is true. You don't need to sit around moping, girl. You need to get out and explore other avenues."

"Easier said than done. Besides, I don't have any prospects and I'm not rushing to get involved in anything else serious."

"I only want you to be open."

"Why are you so eager for me to meet knew people?"

"Not people.... Diandre."

"Who?"

"He's a friend of mine I met through Blu."

"Camille, I don't know. You are always trying to play Cupid."

"What do you have to lose, Dezzy? I didn't say you have to commit to the man tomorrow."

"I don't have anything to lose, Camille because I am not having it."

"Look, I told the man you would be over here later this evening. Don't make a liar out of me. I love you, bye!" I heard the dial tone before I could respond. I was about to call her back when I had a recap of the night before. It was then I decided the least I could do was think about it.

I was in the shower letting the water hit me in the face. I grabbed the shower head moments later and let the water massage me all over my body, especially my neck and shoulders – the tensest areas. When the water hit my pleasure spot, it dawned on me I hadn't been touched by a man in an intimate way in a long time. Before long, I found myself adjusting the showerhead and putting one foot up on the edge of the bathtub. It was a damn shame I'd had a man for two years but had to please myself majority of the time. As my body began to quiver, I cried. I didn't understand why I always had such bad luck with men. I stayed selective and tried to avoid drama at all costs but it always seemed to find me... no matter what.

I was walking down 17th street in Downtown Oakland on my way to Showcase Wigs. I had a bit of time to spare before my first client so I was going to have my eyelashes and eyebrows done. My timing was awful because it seemed like every woman in Oakland had the same idea. I only stayed because the outcome was well worth the wait. I walked to the back of the shop, grabbed a number then went to take my seat. The conversations taking place came from all walks of life. I normally would have ignored the conversations but one of them stood out more than the others.

"Girl, yes Keisha Stross. She caught Dre in her bed with another female and snapped!"

"You can't blame the girl. What ever made Dre think he could pull the stunt and get away with it?"

"I know, right? Keisha and that fool have dated for years. Everyone knows she is crazy about him."

"She needs to chill out, though. One of these days her attitude is going to come back to haunt her."

I listened in disgust. It amazed me how so many people immersed themselves in business that didn't concern them. While most of what these girls were saying was true, it wasn't their place to tell. I made a mental note to call Keisha later tonight. My number was called. Minutes later, I was out the door.

I amazed myself. At times like today, my day was so busy I hadn't had an opportunity to break for lunch. I was barely able to squeeze in the restroom. My faithful client and close friend, Robyn, made sure I was taken care of. While waiting to be seen, she ran to Ming's Chinese Food restaurant in Berkeley to get me a small fried rice. When she returned, she had enough food for a family of four. She was carrying twins. She would have no problems inhaling all of the food. Robyn was my last client of the day. By the time she'd finished eating, I was ready. Robyn updated me on all the latest drama between her and her boyfriend. Listening to the happenings in her life, my life didn't seem as chaotic any more. Secretly, I believed Robyn enjoyed all the stress because despite all Trevell did, she continued to stay with him. Now she was going to have his babies. I could only imagine the possibilities. She could do much better. She's very attractive. She was all babies now but when she wasn't pregnant she had a sleek, athletic build, dark curly hair that accented her slender face, and green eyes that still had a tantalizing effect on any man she came across. Trevell was the first man to put it on her and since then she hasn't paid anyone else any attention.

"Girl, I'll be so happy when I have these babies. I'm getting fat and

Trevell ain't really wanting me like he used to."

"Robyn, please you are far from fat."

"Dezzy, do you know how long its been since I had an orgasm?"

"Oh please, let's not go there."

"Zereck, ain't putting it down?"

"Zereck, who?"

"Girl, what happened?"

"Long story."

"I have time!"

"I don't," I laughed. "You're finished and I am past ready to go."

"I'll call you later on tonight. I have to hear this."

"Yeah, yeah."

Once I cleaned my station and locked up, it was six-thirty. I was tired but it was too early to go home on a Saturday night. I contemplated going by Lee's house since I was around the corner but she'd already started her shift at the hospital. This was nothing new. I usually spent my Saturday nights alone but at twenty two years old I shouldn't be living my life like an old maid.

I sat in the car collecting my thoughts. Everyone on East 14th, including the homeless people, seemed like they had somewhere to go. There was no reason for me to be sitting around feeling sorry for myself. There had to be something I could get in to. A young couple walked past my car laughing and cuddling. Before long, I found myself making a right on 55th Avenue. I drove until 55th became MacArthur. I passed by Mills College and jumped on the MacArthur freeway. I had a destination, Camille's house. It was time to move on.

When I pulled up in front of Camille's house, her BMW was the only car in the driveway. Good. I'd beaten him here. I checked my hair and make-up in the mirror and made the necessary adjustments. If this was a waste of my time, Camille was going to hear it.

"Ooh, don't you look cute? I knew your ass wanted to get back into the game."

"Please, I just got off work."

"Whatever, come on in."

Camille is a real estate agent and excellent at her job. She managed to get herself a serious home near Lake Merrit. Because she could afford it, she'd hired professional interior decorators to furnish the house. She always kept it nice, so nice guests were afraid to touch anything. After removing my shoes, I followed her down a mirrored hallway into the living room. She'd made some changes since I'd been over, two months ago. The first change I noticed was the baby grand piano sitting in the corner.

"Camille, why are you frontin' you can't play the piano."

"Girl, not even a little bit. Blu plays, it's his."

"You and Blu are getting pretty serious."

"I like to think so but his ass is still afraid of commitment."

"What man isn't?"

"Okay?"

In addition to the piano, the walls had been painted sea foam green and were trimmed with ivory. The design on her new Brocade furniture followed the same color scheme. Her living room was spacious. She made it an issue not to over crowd it. I admired her sense of style.

"Have a seat, Dezzy. Do you want a drink?"

"What do you have?"

"Too many to name. How about I fix you a Vodka and cranberry juice?"

"That's cool."

"I'll be right back."

I was looking at Camille's book collection when the doorbell rang. I felt myself become nervous. My heart started pounding and I would swear I could actually feel the blood rushing through my veins. I was mad at myself for getting all worked up behind someone I didn't know. He could turn out to be everything wrong in a man. After all, Camille had told me nothing about him. She only insisted we meet. I held my breath as I heard two pairs of footsteps get closer to the living room. I hurried and picked up a book to look as though I had been busy and was the least bit anxious. I was facing the window so I didn't see him when they came in.

"Dezzy," Camille giggled. I knew she was referring to my poor attempt at looking busy. "This is Diandre."

I turned to acknowledge him and was blown away. This man was – immaculate. "And Diandre this is, Dezzy." His lips parted revealing a beautiful smile. "How are you doing, Dezzy?"

"It's nice to meet you, Diandre."

He was dark chocolate with a muscular build. He stood about six foot two – very nice to my five foot three. His eyes were big, brown and hypnotizing. His lips were inviting. He was nicely manicured, a fresh fade, tapered goatee, and fashionably dressed. He wore a black and gray Enyce sweater, black denim jeans and Lugz – size thirteen, easy. Diandre presented himself as what I like to call a mannerable roughneck.

"Here's your drink, Dezzy. Would you like something to drink, Diandre?"

"Do you have any Hennessey?" Definitely a roughneck.

"You are Blu's boy. He should have some left." Camille left the room. Diandre turned his attention back to me.

"What were you reading?"

"Oh, Camille has Terry McMillan's most recent novel. I haven't read it yet. I was reading the back to see what it was about."

"*A Day Late, and a Dollar Short?*"

"That's the one! You're familiar with Terry McMillan?"

"I have all of her books."

"Really? I'm impressed."

"How else am I supposed to know how to treat women? I don't want Terry talking about my black ass in her next novel."

We both laughed. Good. This wasn't going to be as hard as I thought. Camille came back long enough to give Diandre his drink then she was gone. I took my drink and sat on the window seat. He grabbed a coaster and sat down at the piano.

"You play?"

"No. Blu is the one with all the talent. I'm the man behind the music.

Oh, boy. Another man in the music industry. Give him a chance, Dezzy.

"A producer?"

"Yeah, I like to think of myself as one."

"How long have you been in the business?"

"Are you trying to figure out my age?"

"No, I'd ask."

"Seven years."

"Age?" I asked, smiling.

"Twenty-nine... too old?"

"Not at all."

"Good."

Time passed and we covered a lot of ground: our aspirations, goals, hobbies, you name it. So far, so good. Diandre and I had much in common. Though we'd just met, it seemed like we went back years. We had been so wrapped up in one another we didn't notice when Blu entered the room. His demeanor was similar to that of Diandre's, nonchalant and serious at the same time. Blu acknowledged me first then walked over to Diandre. They talked business for a moment then Diandre subtly told Blu he wasn't there to see him. Taking the hint, Blu left to find Camille.

"Dezzy, you want to get out of here and go somewhere else?"

"What did you have in mind?"

"I'm down for whatever, baby."

"Lake Merrit is beautiful at night if you can get past the smell."

"Sounds good. I can follow you in my car."

"Let me say goodbye to my cousin then we can go."

We lucked up on two parking spaces across from Gold's Gym. It was colder than I thought it would be. Diandre went into the trunk of his Mercedes and handed me his leather coat – such the gentleman. I put on the oversized coat then we began our stroll around the lake. People kept looking at us together. One older man actually told us we were an attractive couple. I blushed and Diandre didn't bother to correct him. The moonlit, star-filled sky capped off my first romantic Saturday night in a long time. With all of our talking and laughing, it didn't seem like we'd walked over a three mile stretch. In fact, I hadn't realized until we were back in front of our cars.

"Well, Diandre I had a very nice time tonight."

"Well, if you did why are you making the night sound so final?"

"Not my intention at all."

"Good. Is it safe to ask for your number?"

"Only if I can have yours in return."

"Baby, you ain't said anything but a word. I have it made out for you already."

"Oh, you know your game is that tight?"

"Not game, Dezzy... confidence."

I handed him his coat. He walked with me to the driver's side of my car. I got in and rolled down the window to continue talking. "Good night, Diandre."

"What about your number?"

"Come on now, you expect me to believe my Cupid cousin didn't supply my information?"

"You know her far too well."

"I know."

"Drive safely."

"I will."

I waited for Diandre to get into his car. Once he was inside, I pulled away from the curb. I decided to take another route home. I was tired of routine and Diandre was the first change.

Chapter Three

The next morning I awoke to male voices coming from the kitchen. I didn't bother throwing on my robe. I recognized one of the voices and was immediately on the defense — my appearance didn't matter. I stormed into the kitchen and saw Zereck talking with my brother.

"Dezzy, Zereck dropped by on his way to the studio. I was on my way to come and get you."

"What are you doing here?" I completely ignored my brother.

"I came to see you, can we talk? We need to get some things straight."

"What is there to straighten out, Zereck? You cheated and got caught, end of story."

"Can't I at least explain?"

"Zereck, if you really wanted to explain yourself you would have done it then, not three days later. I told you I don't want anything else to do with you. I've moved on, now leave."

"Moved on? That's bullshit. You ain't messing with any other niggas."

"I'm done talking to you, Zereck."

"Dezzy!"

"Look, my sister has spoken. Pick your sorry ass jaw up off of the floor and step. I'd hate to have to kick your ass."

Zereck eyeballed me long and hard before finally leaving. How dare he have the audacity to come to my house after the stunt he pulled. It's my own fault. He and I had problems before and I always accepted his sorry apologies. He thought he would be able to bring me flowers and a tired speech about how he'd messed up thinking it would be all good — not any more.

"So that's what wasn't bothering you?"

"Yeah."

"You know, I could have handled him if you needed me to."

"Yeah, I know."

I pulled the curtains back and opened all the windows in my room. The cool morning breeze rushed in. It dried the tears on my cheeks quicker than I could wipe them away. Realizing I'd cried my last cry, I had a sudden burst of energy. I began a

27

long-awaited, thorough cleaning of my room. I turned on my stereo and put the dial on KBLX, better know as the Quiet Storm. I cranked up the volume as "People Make the World Go 'Round" by The Stylistics leaked through my speakers. I've been told I have an old soul. That's true to an extent. I can appreciate good music. I like music, old and new, it's therapeutic. In fact, music had helped me through numerous tough times. It would help me through this too. I never realized all the memorabilia I had of my relationship with Zereck until I began discarding it. If I was truly going to move on, I didn't need anything making the change difficult. I looked at everything — cards, pictures, clothes — one final time before heaving it all into a large green garbage bag. Already, a burden had been lifted off of my shoulders.

Two hours later my room was spotless. Opium incents filled my room and Luther Vandross filled my soul. I put the last of my laundry away and was sitting in the middle of my floor appreciating the free moment. Before long, Diandre floated into my mind. So far, so good. He almost seemed too good to be true but he could very well be the man I'd been waiting on. There I go jumping ahead of myself. I don't even know the man — give it time, Dezzy.

Keisha's answering machine came on and I was relieved. Of course I was concerned about my friend's well-being but at the same time I didn't want to be consumed with someone else's drama. I only wanted to keep my word. My message was short and to the point. After I hung up, I pushed Keisha into my subconscious. No sooner than I put the phone on the base, my cell phone rang. I didn't recognize the number. Against the norm, I answered anyway.

"Did I catch you at a bad time?"

"No, Diandre. Now is as good a time as any." Camille had given him my cell phone number. She knew better.

"You sound like you're sleeping."

"I'm relaxing. How are you?"

"I'm fine... look, Dezzy, I realize we were together last night but I'd like to see you today."

"I'd like that. I am far from dressed, though."

"There is no need to rush. What time should I pick you up?"

"You can meet me at Camille's house in an hour and a half."

"Oh, I must need to earn more brownie points before I make it to the crib."

"Exactly," I laughed.

"Well, I'll see you at three-thirty."

"See you shortly."

Camille sat on Blu's lap while he and Diandre had a beer on the porch. One of them mentioned something funny because now everyone was laughing. An older white couple quickly passed with their dog making certain they didn't look in their direction. Diandre noticed me first. He sat down his beer and walked over to my car. We talked for a moment before Camille walked up next to him.

"Dezzy, at least get out of the car, girl."

"No need to get comfortable, Dezzy. I want us to get going before it gets too dark."

"Where are we going?"

"Don't ask questions, you'll see."

"Should I follow you in my car or do you want me to ride?"

"Oh I want you to ride, no doubt, but I don't mind driving."

He looked me in my eyes. There was no need to speak. Camille suddenly did an about face and walked away. I laughed. I waited for Diandre to move his car out of Camille's driveway then I parked my car in its place. I said my goodbyes and moments later we were off.

Diandre drove fast but I didn't feel threatened. The sunroof was open and the windows down. I lowered my Gucci sunglasses and sat back as the wind blew through my hair. He used the remote to skip through the CDs until he landed on Roger and Zapp. Seconds later, I felt the vibrations of "Computer Love" throughout my entire body. Now I was comfortable as we headed east on the MacArthur freeway.

After winding up a narrow road surrounded by towering trees and overbearing bushes, we came into a clearing where a log cabin sat alone. Rose bushes sat on either side and there was a deck complete with a gazebo overlooking a man-made lake. The place was beautiful. The inside of the cabin was even more compelling. The furniture was old-fashioned with a touch of modern. There was a fireplace in the living room and both bedrooms. The kitchen was spacious. It had a black and silver theme. The bathroom was the best. It had a self-standing tub and toilet with a flushing lever. The thick gray carpet felt good on my bare feet once I'd taken off my shoes and sat down on the couch. On his insistence, I rested there while he brought bags of groceries inside. While I waited, I called my brother and let him know I would be home extremely late, if at all, then I turned off my phone all together.

"Do you like seafood?"

"You can cook too?"

"I have to cook. There isn't anyone to do it for me."

"What's on the menu?"

"Shrimp and prawns... do you approve?"

"Do what you do, boo. Is there anything I can help you with?"

"If you can handle the salad, I can handle the rest."

"Deal."

"The cabinet above the television is a mini-bar if you want a drink."

"Thank you. I may see what you're working with a little later."

"I hope so."

The aroma had my mouth salivating so I was more than ready when we sat down to the candlelit dinner for two. Diandre was as hungry as I was because there was little conversation. Once we'd finished, I restored the kitchen while Diandre watched the end of SportsCenter. I was putting the leftovers in the refrigerator when the scent of Drakkar engulfed my nostrils. I turned around to see Diandre standing there with his shirt off. I fought hard with myself to hold my mouth shut. I won. I stood with my back against the refrigerator unable to move as he walked towards me. He pierced my eyes with his then kissed me gently on my neck. I was screaming on the inside because I couldn't believe this was happening. It had been far too long. He pulled back, looked at me again, then kissed me softly on my lips. I'm not sure if I returned the kiss. I was in a trance. When I opened my eyes, Diandre had me by my hand leading me into the master bedroom. It didn't matter Diandre and I hadn't known one another for years on end. I longed to be touched by a man and now it was going to happen. He made sure the experience was memorable for us both. He removed my blouse and bra then instructed me to lie down on my stomach. Moments later, warm oil trickled down the dip of my back. His hands were strong and gentle as I received my massage. I laid there helpless as he removed the rest of my clothing. He began exploring every inch of my body with his tongue while removing his own clothes. I waited patiently while he wrestled with a condom wrapper then braced myself as he entered my body. Diandre moved with slow, strategic motions making me savor every moment. It wasn't long before we both reached the moment of ecstasy — in unison.

Diandre was still asleep when I got up to shower. I didn't have a change of clothes so I pulled one of his t-shirts out of the drawer. While I toweled off in the bathroom, I could hear Diandre on the phone. I slid on the t-shirt and quietly came out of the bathroom. Women's intuition told me he was on the phone with a female but my gut told me not to jump to any conclusions. I heard him telling the female he couldn't talk because he was busy, timing was bad, and this wasn't the place. I waited for him to hang up then went and stood in the doorway of the living room. Diandre didn't see me right away.

"Hey, Dezzy." He was nervous.

"Hello."

"Did you hear a lot?"

"Enough." I hadn't heard anything but Diandre was feeling guilty, he'd talk.

"Look, I can't lie to you. That was a friend... well more than a friend. I have a son from a previous relationship. I was talking to his mother."

"A son... why didn't you mention him before?"

"I didn't want to scare you off before anything could get started."

"Diandre, I told you communication is key with me."

"Better late than never, right?" He was nonchalant.

"How old is he?"

"Two."

"A baby."

"Don't be mad, baby. I'll tell you whatever you want to know."

"How about you tell me what you think I *should* know."

"There's nothing else to tell, I swear."
"Well, okay... I guess."
"Are you mad?"
"No. I'm going to bed."
"Right... we have to get up early so you're back in time for work."

There was no need to tell him I didn't work on Mondays. I wanted to be home as early as possible. I was going to need plenty of time to rethink this one. Diandre climbed in bed with me after his shower. He attempted to pull me close but I turned my back. He got the message.

The ride back to Camille's house was uncomfortable. Diandre and I talked but it was obvious both of us were trying to fill the awkward silence. I was upset with Diandre for his lack of communication but I didn't want to appear as though I was completely bent out of shape. A child was not the end of the world, the world only became more complicated. If Diandre and I continued to occupy one another's time, this woman and I would cross paths. I would get over it. I was overwhelmed right now. When we pulled up in front of Camille's house, I gave him a kiss before getting in my car. My intentions were to put his mind at ease, for the time being.

Lee's Altima was parked in front of my house when I arrived. My gut told me something was wrong. Lee never came over this early. Lord, please don't let there be anything wrong with my mother. I rushed through the door. Donte was sitting with Lee who had a box of Kleenex in her lap.

"Lee, what's wrong? Donte, is mama okay?"

"Mama's fine."

"What is it then?"

"It's Kei... Keisha's dead. She was killed."

Chapter Four

There are some things in life I will never understand. I am not supposed to be in Rolling Hills Memorial Park watching a childhood friend be lowered into the ground. I was leaving a message on her machine a week ago not realizing it would be the last. I'm most baffled by the circumstances surrounding her sudden death. She loved too hard. All she wanted was to be loved in return. Instead, her obsession with a need to be loved by a man resulted in her demise. I can't imagine being so engrossed in a man one loses sight of herself. Keisha's death is proof it's possible. I can learn from her example – love cannot be the death of me.

It's really stupid when I think about it. His ego. Her mouth. An embarrassed girl. A bullet. He couldn't get enough, she'd had enough and apparently so did the anonymous female. All I can do now is pray justice is served. What's done is done, the past can't be changed. Initially, it will be hard but life goes on.

The time I spent alone in my room made me realize how loud silence really is. I hadn't been motivated to do anything. Keisha was still running through my mind. I knew mourning wouldn't solve anything. Keisha would want me to go on but I felt moving on would be selfish. As quickly as the thought entered my mind, it had gone. My phone rang interrupting my thoughts. As if Robyn had been reading my mind, she called to invite me out for a day of shopping. Her reasoning made sense. If we stayed busy there was less time to sit around and be depressed. Trusting her judgment, I quickly agreed.

We were in the children's department of Mervyns at Southland Mall looking at baby clothes. We sorted through outfits for boys and girls since Robyn was having one of each. Robyn hadn't stopped talking since we'd stepped foot in the mall. I appreciated the conversation. The highlight of her rambling, and the news that changed my mood, was learning of her recent engagement to Trevell. Regardless of my opinion of the situation, Robyn was honestly happy and that was all that mattered. Since we had nothing but time on our hands, I told Robyn about the now nonexistent Zereck and my new male interest, Diandre. Being Robyn, she had a million questions and I answered them with no hesitance. I was so involved in my discussion of Diandre, I hadn't noticed the female standing near me watching my every move and listening intently.

"So you're the bitch Diandre has been spending all of his time with?"

"Excuse me?"

"You heard me. You are not all that. How much ass are you giving up to the point he doesn't want to spend time with his own son?"

"Now you wait one damn minute. You have nerve coming at me like this. I'm not stopping Diandre from seeing his son and you know it. I know one thing, though, if you ever come at me like this again I will break your foot off in your ass. Do we have an understanding?"

"Watch your back, bitch. I will get him back."

"Robyn, I'm done here. Are you ready to go?"

"Lead the way."

This was not about Diandre. I would never fight over a man. This was about being disrespected. Regardless of the way she may have felt, I could have been approached differently. Robyn and I made our purchases and left. I had a strong desire to go back and really let her have it but I was going to be the bigger woman. She was not my problem. Diandre would have to deal with this.

Robyn and I were having burgers at Nations in Hayward while talking about her upcoming wedding. She was wasting no time. Her babies were due in two months; her wedding would be in four. The excitement was all throughout Robyn's eyes as she spoke. The next few weeks would be hectic for all parties involved but I had no doubts Robyn would be able to pull it off.

Robyn was discussing her potential wedding party when a group of loud females walked into the restaurant. They drew attention to themselves by being rowdy and vulgar. Most of the patrons kept to themselves and attempted to ignore them, Robyn and I included. One of the females ordered for the group then the entire bunch came and sat at the booth directly across from us. Robyn began discussing color schemes as the rift-raft engaged in their own conversation.

"Shit, Dre should be happy Keisha's off his hands. All he did was complain to me all the time anyway."

"Keshonda, you did what you had to do. The bitch was flapping off at the mouth. She couldn't keep disrespecting you."

"That's right, the bitch didn't recognize so I had to let her know."

Robyn and I sat frozen, listening. I wanted to believe I was hallucinating and had totally misunderstood the girl but the expression on Robyn's face confirmed everything. I wished there was something I could do but I was helpless. There was one of me – Robyn's pregnant – and six of them. If I attempted to do anything, I was certain I would become a statistic too. I couldn't go to the police, I didn't have proof. Besides, where I'm from if I decided to snitch I might as well have planned my funeral too. I turned to get a good look at the female speaking in order to have a mental picture then Robyn and I packed up. I don't know how but we managed to stand up and walk out of the restaurant. My mind raced with methods of retaliation. Somehow, justice would have to be served.

I could feel the tears welling up in my eyes as Robyn pulled into my driveway. A day designed to make me feel better only made me feel worse. Just as I thought I was beginning to deal with Keisha's death, I cross her murderer – what are the odds? Robyn, who had been in a trance since we'd left, muttered what I assumed to be comforting words then she drove off. Those girls would pay but only time would tell.

No one was home but I still went to my room. I needed to clear my head. While I often wrote in my journal to escape my problems, I occasionally preferred a method which required little effort. I locked my bedroom door then went into my bathroom and snatched my bath towel off of the rack. I saturated it with water in the bathtub, rung it out, and placed it across the half-inch space under my bedroom door. Next, I pulled back my curtains and opened both windows – Jack Frost was biting but I didn't care. I walked over to my bookshelf and pushed half the volume of Encyclopedias to the side exposing a wooden pencil box which sat farther back. Inside, was an eighth of marijuana and two pre-rolled joints. I removed one of the joints then replaced the bookshelf as it had been. No one knew about this habit, not even my brother. My incents of choice this time were Halston. I lit several of them around the room and candles too. I turned on Jill Scott then sat down on my bed. Finally, I placed the joint to my lips and lit away. In a matter of moments I no longer had a care in the world.

I was taking a long walk with Jill when my cell phone rang. Diandre popped up on the caller id. I sat up and attempted to pull myself together before answering the phone. I didn't want to sound the least bit distorted and give myself away. I was glad he'd called. I always liked to hear from him but I was especially eager to tell him about the little run in today with his son's mother. I answered on the fourth ring.

"Oh, I thought I was going to have to leave a message."

"What, you don't want to talk to me?"

"Of course! You took forever to answer your phone, that's all."

"It was at the bottom of my purse," I lied.

"I was calling to check on you. I know you have been through a lot this past week."

"I have and it has been hard at times but I'm strong. I'll bounce back in due time."

"That's my girl. I've been trying to give you your space this last week. It's been hard but I've managed. What have you been doing to keep from going crazy?"

"Not much besides working before today. I went shopping with my girlfriend for baby clothes."

"Baby clothes?"

"No need to be alarmed. She's having twins."

"Oh, okay."

I laughed at Diandre's relief.

"I ran into someone you know at the mall."

"Really, who? How'd you know?"

"She made herself known."

"She?"

"Mmm hmm... it was your son's mother."

"What? Dezzy, did she come at you foul?"

"She tried to but I let her know I wasn't having it."

"What happened?"

"Long story short, she accused me of coming between you and your son. I told her it wasn't true. I said the two of you had issues that didn't concern me then she threatened to get you back."

"She did what? Dezzy, you have nothing to worry about. Justine and I are through. I quit her ass a year ago."

"Diandre, I'm secure in me. I'm not worried about it. As far as me coming between you and your son–"

"Say no more, Dezzy. I'm tired of this shit. Let me call you back."

"I'm not going anywhere."

I gave Diandre my home telephone number before letting him off of the phone. I believed I'd done right by telling him. If the issue wasn't addressed in the beginning, it would definitely be an ongoing problem. I only hoped Diandre's phone call would be all that was necessary.

I was floating on cloud nine when I heard the front door close. My brother and his girlfriend were talking in the living room. I knew it would only be a short matter of time before my brother came up to my room after seeing my El Dorado in the driveway. I wasn't sure if I'd camouflaged the weed smell in my bedroom so I put Visine in my eyes, sprayed perfume on my neck and wrists then went downstairs to my brother before he could come to me.

"D, I'm so glad you're home. Raijean and I have something to tell you."

I had no idea what my brother was going to say. Granted, Raijean was the first girlfriend I'd known my brother to be completely faithful, I wasn't convinced he was ready for marriage.

"What Donte?"

"Rai, do you want to tell her?"

"Dezzy, you're going to be an auntie!"

"Wait, what did you just say?"

"D, we're having a baby!"

"Whoa, uh... congratulations"

"Thanks, Dezzy... mama is going to be shocked."

"I'll say... well, I heard you two come in. I only came down to say hey. I'm going to make myself a bowl of cereal. I'll leave you two alone. D, I'll be upstairs if you need me... congratulations, again."

"Thanks," they said in unison.

Munchies are a trip. If I'm not careful, I'll be the size of a house. This is the reason I smoke in moderation. I'd finished off a pack of Beef Jerky and began popping Sunflower Seeds. I was full before the bowl of cereal but I couldn't control the hunger. I knew if I continued eating, my high would come down – I stopped.

Lee had me on hold for five minutes but it felt like an eternity. She had to take the other call; it was her job. At times, Lee's job as a registered nurse totally consumed her. She seldom made time for herself let alone a man. Her last boyfriend couldn't handle the demands of her career so he left before anything serious could get off of the ground. This was our topic of conversation.

"Okay... I'm back. I'm sorry about that."

"Lee, we both know the right man is going to come along. He will be a man who isn't intimidated by your independence."

"I'm beginning to wonder about these fools I've been coming across. I'm starting to lose faith in black men."

"What? Lee, I've never heard you talk like this before."

"I don't want to but the grass is looking greener on the other side."

"Lee, you can't be-" my line beeped, "hold on a minute."

"No, D you go ahead and take your call. I need to prepare for work tomorrow."

"Call me later?"

"I will." Click.

"Hello?"

"Dezzy, it's me. I talked to Justine. She won't be bothering you anymore."

"Is everything all right?"

"Everything is fine. Would you like to come over?"

"Over where?"

"Here."

"Now?"

"Uh, yeah. That's what I had in mind when I asked you."

"Are you sure?"

"Positive. I'm not keeping track of brownie points," he chuckled.

Diandre gave me directions to his house in Fremont. Judging by the fact it was already eleven o'clock, this would be an overnight trip. I showered, did my hair, put on light make up then put on a red bra and thong set. There was nothing wrong with providing my man with a little eye candy. I sprayed Carolina Herrera on all of my private places – behind the ears, on the neck, wrists, cleavage, navel, and of course on my inner thighs. I prepared a quick overnight bag before putting on my three-inch red Stilettos. I grabbed my black three-quarter length leather jacket and tied the belt. The coat was all the clothes I needed to wear. I left a note for my brother and was on the Nimitz freeway in no time.

Diandre's neighborhood was gorgeous and serene; his house exquisite. His two-story home was gray and white with a two car garage. Pebble stoned concrete led up to his front French doors. His manicured lawn was outlined with small lantern-styled lights. The mailbox stood alone in front of the house. I pulled next to his Mercedes sitting in the driveway and a censored light came on. I popped my trunk, grabbed my bag and walked to the front door. As I knocked, the door slowly crept open. I expected to find Diandre standing there. Instead, I found a pile of rose petals and a note which read: "Find Me!"

Tickled inside, I closed and locked the door behind me. I gently sat my bag on the floor then proceeded with the hunt. I went through several rooms with no luck before heading upstairs. As my foot touched the top step, "Between the Sheets" by the Isley Brothers began to play through ceiling speakers. I tried to contain my excitement but there was no denying the new found pep-in-my-step. Three doorways stood before me, excluding the bathroom. To my left was a room decorated with Disney characters, obviously his son's room. Diagonal and to my right was what I assumed to be the guest room. Straight ahead, the door was closed but the candlelight flickers coming from underneath exposed Diandre's hiding place. I turned the knob slowly.

Diandre stood in front of his bed wearing black silk pajamas and holding a single rose. Candles outlined the room and rose petals were scattered generously across his bed. On his nightstand sat a bucket of ice with champagne and two flute glasses. He picked up a remote control and lowered the music playing above our heads.

"You found me."

"Indeed, I did."

"Make yourself at home."

"I intend to."

Diandre sat on the foot of his bed and waited while I removed my coat. A look of surprise and pleasure swept across his face as my coat fell to the floor.

"Oh, I know you didn't think you were the only person with tricks up your sleeve."

I stood before him with one hand on my hip and put on my sexy game face. Being a woman, I knew how to push his buttons. I sauntered over to Diandre and stood in-between his legs. He stroked my face, unfastened my bra, and then buried his face in my chest. I was in the mood to play so I backed away in an attempt to make him work harder. He stood, and to my surprise removed his pajamas. Instead of moving towards me, he climbed onto his bed and sprawled out on his back. I took my time walking over to the bed. Rather than join him, I reached into the bucket on the nightstand and removed a piece of ice. I ran the ice across his lips, nipples, and navel. I wanted him to yearn for it. He did. Diandre's personally designed CD switched from "Between the Sheets" to "Freakin' You" by Jodeci. My thong nearly melted off. I removed my thong but the Stilettos weren't going anywhere. Sensing my intentions, Diandre removed a condom from under the pillow and put it on. I stood over him on the bed. He caressed my legs. Becoming impatient, he grabbed me behind both knees causing my legs to buckle. As I lowered myself onto him, the phone began ringing. Diandre didn't bother to pause and neither did I. The entire moment was ruined when Justine began talking on the answering machine.

"Diandre, I know you're in there with her. She can't love you like I can, baby. What do you see in her? She can't do anything for you. She's a child. I love-"

"Don't call my muthaphuckin' house disrespecting people. Who do you think you are? You don't run a damn thing over here... and you wonder why I dumped your tired ass. You are too damn immature. Don't call my house anymore unless it has something to do with my son."

I took the receiver out of his hand and placed it in its cradle. My mood was ruined, and Diandre was pissed. For a woman who believed she could win him back, she was only successful at pushing Diandre away. He sat up on the bed and held his head in his hands. I rubbed his back as we sat in silence. Out of nowhere, he stood up, grabbed his robe and walked out the bedroom. I didn't take his actions personally, he wasn't upset with me. I figured he wanted time to himself, I would grant him that right.

I was showering in Diandre's personal oversized bathroom. I could hear him and Justine arguing on the telephone again. I had no idea what they were arguing about this time around, I only hoped it would end soon. I took my time preparing for bed. When I walked out into his bedroom, Diandre sat in a chair near the window fully clothed.

"Dezzy, I need to go and get my son. Do you mind hanging out here until I get back?"

"No, I don't mind. Are you sure you don't want me to go with you?"

"No, I'm going to deal with this by myself. I know how to handle Justine. If you came with me, it would only make everything more difficult... I mean you're not a problem but–"

"Don't try to explain, Diandre... go and get your baby."

Even though Diandre was trying to be kind, I knew I was the reason all this drama was going on. Justine was already putting strain on our relationship. Diandre wants to move forward with his life but he values the relationship he has with his son and that's understandable. What will it take to make her understand?

While he was gone, I used his phone. I had to tell someone about all the drama that, once again, managed to find me. There was no answer at Camille's and Lee was sure to be dead to the world at this hour. I ended up calling my cousin Katryna. She was very cut-throat and said whatever was on her mind. She'd had a hard upbringing. She didn't care about anyone but family – extended family. Katryna and I weren't blood-related but our close-knit friendship stemmed from childhood. I considered her blood. I loved her to death but her crazy ways was one of the very reasons why we didn't spend more time together. I had to be careful because people often assume birds-of-a-feather-flock-together. I knew deep down she was a good person which was the only reason I continued to deal with her. It had been a while since we'd saw one another so once we'd finished talking we made arrangements to get together the next day. I was hanging up the phone as Diandre walked through the door. I expected to meet his son but he was alone.

"Where's your son?"

"After all the bullshit, she wouldn't let me see him."

"That's not right."

"She said some shit about me not being a good father figure."

"I know it's easier said than done, Diandre but don't let this stress you. I'm sure she'll come around."

"Yeah, she better before I have to."

Chapter Five

When Lee and I pulled in front of Katryna's apartment building, she was standing on her balcony drinking an Old English beer while having a conversation with someone she knew across the street. I swallowed hard. From her slurred speech, I could tell she was loaded and I knew how she could get. If she hadn't seen me already, I would have left. I was regretting this day and it hadn't started. I pulled in the driveway in front of a spray-painted sign which read: "No Parkin' Any Tyme." Katryna didn't have a car but she didn't want anyone parking in her space. Lee waited in the car while I headed up the stairwell to Katryna's door. "Baddest Bitch" by Trina was blasting inside her apartment. The door was opened for me to come inside, I did. Katryna stumbled around grabbing her belongings and making sure everything was turned off. When she headed for the door, I followed suit.

Once we came to the car, Lee had moved into the backseat out of respect for Katryna. Lee didn't know her but that's the type of woman Lee is. I introduced them and Katryna failed to acknowledge her. I knew Lee wasn't worried about Katryna's lack of manners but I was embarrassed. At this point, I could only hope Katryna would remove the stick up her ass before we got to Robyn's house. I told her ahead of time I would be meeting friends to help plan a wedding. She agreed to come along.

Robyn purchased every bridal magazine created. After three hours, they all looked the same to me. I wasn't complaining I was enjoying all the preparation. It made me look forward to the day I tied the knot but I am in no rush. We took a break to enjoy the lasagna, garlic bread, and salad Robyn prepared for everyone – Katryna stepped outside. A friend of Robyn's commented on our choices of bridal gowns accusing Robyn of making sure she was the only one getting attention during the ceremony. We all laughed knowing it was said in fun. Everyone knew our dresses would be stunning. Katryna walked back inside as Lee teased Robyn about wearing a white dress. Everyone laughed again since she'd raised a valid point.

"That shit ain't funny." Katryna said.

"Uh, Katryna... what's wrong with you," I asked.

Her eyes were bloodshot and her clothes reeked of marijuana. Being an undercover smoker, I knew she was high. I wished I could crawl under a rock.

"Your bitch ass God Sister."

"Look, I didn't do anything to you, and I ain't going to be too many more bitches."

"Fuck you!"

"Excuse me?"

Lee sat her plate on the coffee table. She stood up, straightened her clothes then planted herself directly in front of Katryna.

"Dezzy, check your cousin before I have to."

"What are you going to do you sadiddy bi–"

My words were caught in my throat. I knew I'd seen it with my own eyes but I didn't want to believe my God Sister had jabbed Katryna in her jaw.

"You bitch!" Katryna yelled as she hurled Lee backwards into a bookcase.

I couldn't believe these two women were fighting in Robyn's house. They were far too old and the reason wasn't worth the time. Camille and I rushed over pulling them apart while everyone else sat in shock.

"What the hell is wrong with you Katryna?" I asked in disbelief.

I was trembling with anger. I couldn't believe Katryna would embarrass me this way. It was obvious her self image didn't matter. She had never met any of my friends and this was not the way to make a first impression. Lee apologized to Robyn for disrespecting her house then walked into the kitchen to get ice for her hand. Robyn wobbled over to Katryna and demanded she leave her house.

"I don't care, I'll leave! Are you coming, Dezzy?"

"Look, Katryna I know you're family but I have to go with Robyn on this one. The whole time you've been here you were disrespectful. You are too grown to act like you don't have sense when you get around other people. I honestly thought you may have changed but you have proved me a fool. I will always have love for you Katryna but if you leave the decision to me, you can see yourself home. I love you but I'm sorry. When you learn how to act, call me."

Katryna started towards the door. Before leaving, she turned back and gave me a look of disgust and despair. My heart was hurting but I had to stand my grounds. My entire body flinched when she slammed the door.

"Dezzy, your cous–"

"Don't worry, Robyn. It will never happen again."

Although Robyn said it was unnecessary, I continued to apologize until I went home. Robyn knew Katryna's actions were a reflection of her character, not mine. It would be a while, if at all, before Katryna and I did anything again. I intended to forget this day ever happened. I hoped everyone at Robyn's house would do the same.

I was asleep before my head hit the pillow. After the day's events, I was exhausted. I intended to go by Diandre's house and rekindle the flame from the night before but I didn't have the energy – a first for me. Besides, I was finding myself developing feelings for Diandre that went deeper than the surface. It was nice to have a love interest but intimidating at the same time. I enjoy his company and cherish the moments we spend together but space is important too. Any successful relationship requires each individual to have time to oneself. I didn't want Diandre to feel smothered and I needed air to breathe as well. Truthfully, I didn't want to get too attached to this man and develop false hopes for what could be if there wasn't going to be anything at all – time would unveil destiny.

It was two o'clock in the morning when my phone rang. I felt around in the dark before finally lifting the phone to my ear. I didn't speak. I waited for the explanation of the dire emergency. There had to be one to get a call at this hour. If not, someone was about to hear my mouth because the sleep I rarely get was too good.

"Dezzy?"

My anger subsided and delight took over. Diandre was thinking about me. I was on his mind heavy enough he'd decided to call.

"I'm going to let you off of the hook because it's you. I want you to know, though, you were five seconds from being cursed out."

"Well, we wouldn't want you cursing me out."

"What's up?"

"Well, since you forgot how to use the phone, I thought I'd refresh your memory."

"I didn't forget. I was giving you your space."

"Space? I'm sorry. Tell me when we had an argument, again?"

"We didn't."

"So who told you I needed space?"

"I assu–"

"Stop right there. I'm sure I don't have to tell you the saying."

"No, I'm aware." I chuckled.

"Good... well, while you were out giving space you missed my birthday."

"What? Baby... shit, I did. I'm sorry."

"Yeah, yeah... you would've known if you called."

"Okay, Diandre," I laughed. "I'm sorry I didn't call you. It won't happen again."

"It better not."

"So how can I make it up to you?"

"Blu's throwing me a party at Camille's house–"

"Does my cousin know about this? I mean, the way she is about her furni–"

"Yes, Dezzy she knows. It was her idea. Anyway, it's this Saturday. You can make it up to me by being there."

"Oh is that it? I'll be there."

"Yes, that's all I'm asking for but I have no doubts you'll find another way to repay me."

"Oh, check you out."

"Get some sleep, baby. I'll talk to you tomorrow."

"Goodnight."

Now I was kicking myself. How could I be so wrapped up I forgot his birthday? Diandre didn't seem too disturbed. It was water under the bridge now. I'd have to make it up to him. I'm sure my final decision won't have any objections.

I'd arrived at Camille's house at ten o'clock Saturday morning to help her rearrange her house for the flock of people who would invade her home nine hours later. Because Diandre was a good friend of Blu, he and

Camille were going all out for Diandre's thirtieth birthday. Camille's backyard had been converted into an outdoor nightclub, complete with a bar, café tables with candles, a hardwood dance floor surrounding the pool, and an elevated disc jockey booth. The catered food would arrive closer to the start of the party.

I'd taken the liberty in bringing my clothes for the party with me so I wouldn't have to commute all the way back to Hayward before the party. I showered in the guest bathroom and began to prepare mentally and physically for the evening ahead. I worked on my hair first. After twenty minutes of staring at myself in the mirror, I decided on an up 'do with free falling curls. My attire for the night consisted of a figure-flattering, brown and ivory A-line, spaghetti-strapped rayon dress. I set the outfit off with a pair of brown Fendi sandals. The dress code for the night wasn't formal but everyone was to dress to impress.

People began arriving but I continued to take my time. I wanted to make sure my appearance was flawless. After all, I would be on the arm of the man of honor. I had to be the shit. I didn't know he'd arrived until he knocked on the bedroom door. I checked myself over once more before opening the door. He stood before me in a cream, form-fitting, v-necked sweater, brown slacks and brown and white Stacey Adams – we'd coordinated our colors earlier during the week. Seeing Diandre made my heart flutter. We'd both been busy the past week, relying solely on the telephone to communicate with one another. I was certain Diandre approved of my appearance because I had to close his mouth. I gave him a kiss, closed the bedroom door, put my arm through his and together we walked into the cool night breeze to join the party.

Of all the people at the party, I knew a handful personally. I wasn't worried. I could adapt to any situation or surrounding. I strolled around with Diandre before splitting up and mingling solo. He was having a good time and I was glad. I spotted Lee batting her eyes at the bartender and decided to join her.

"Kevin, this is Dezzy, my God Sister. She's the one I mentioned earlier, a beautician by day and novelist by night."

"It's nice to meet you, Dezzy. I was telling Leeann my uncle has his own publishing company. Have you given thought to publishing your work?"

"Honestly, it's a hobby. I'm not sure how people would receive it."

"You can't live for other people. Besides, Leeann tells me your work is compelling. I'll tell you what, here's my uncle's number. Give the idea some more thought and if you change your mind mention my name and he'll hook you up."

He handed me a napkin with the number scribbled down. I wasn't carrying my purse so I turned my back to them and secured the number deep in my cleavage.

"Thanks a lot, Kevin. We'll see what happens. Can I trouble you for a Midori Sour?"

"You got it."

I chatted with Lee while he fixed the drink. Once he'd finished, I took my drink and left them alone while I worked the room. I was chatting with a radio executive when the disc jockey beckoned Diandre to the booth over the microphone. He demanded everyone join in the singing of the

Stevie Wonder version of "Happy Birthday" as Blu and the caterers escorted out the two-tier birthday cake. Once Diandre made his wish and cut the cake, he snatched the microphone and announced he needed to get his birthday groove on and I was to join him. I was a bit embarrassed but I complied without hesitance. Diandre took my hand in his as "Luv U Better" by LL Cool J began, a personal favorite. I casually got my groove on while making sure I remained a lady. I was putting all my moves on Diandre and he kept up with little effort. We danced the night away stopping only when guests interrupted to announce their departure. Before long, Camille's house was back in order. Diandre and I said our goodbyes then headed to Fremont – it was now time for the private party.

We had been talking and dancing in front of the fireplace to "The Closer I Get to You" by Roberta Flack when Diandre began to kiss me. I was putty in his hands. It took no time before he began lowering the straps of my dress. As he did, the napkin Kevin gave me earlier fell from my chest. I thought nothing of it. Diandre didn't take it so lightly.

"What's this?"

"A number I was given at the party. Why?"

"You were flirting with other niggas?"

"Baby, it's not even like that."

"Well, explain it to me," his voice was firm.

"Diandre, you need to chill out. The number was given to me for business purposes."

"Business my ass."

I lifted the straps back onto my shoulders. The mood was ruined. I couldn't believe we were arguing – behind petty shit.

"Wait a minute, you think I'm lying to you?"

"Are you?"

"Look, I already told you before but if you must know, it's a contact number for a book publisher."

Diandre didn't respond. Instead, he walked in front of the fireplace and tossed the number into the flames. I had to pinch myself to make sure I wasn't having a nightmare.

"What the hell is wrong with you?"

"I have all of the connections you need. All you had to do was tell me you wanted to publish your book. There was no need to go behind my back."

"You know what Diandre, I'm going to leave because if I stay here a minute longer, I'm going to go off. You've went and lost your damn mind. If you're drunk, you need to sleep the shit off and don't call me until you do."

I grabbed my keys and walked out the door, slamming it shut behind me. I was steaming by the time I was inside my car. I couldn't believe the way Diandre was acting, much less how he'd degraded me. My father, a stranger, doesn't have control over me. I'll be damned if I let my man. I hadn't been on the Nimitz freeway five minutes before Diandre began blowing up my cell phone. In the heat of this moment, I didn't want to hear anything he had to say. The ringing ceased for ten minutes and I rode in silence. My mind was racing with solutions to address this problem before it could get any worse. Minutes later, my cell phone began ringing again.

"What?"

I hadn't bothered to look at the caller id. I assumed it was Diandre.

Surprisingly, it was Robyn on the opposite end speaking in a panic. I was barely able to make out what she was saying through the heavy breathing. What I could decipher left me uneasy and my gut suggested I keep my distance. Being a loyal friend, though, I decided to take my chances and help my friend in need.

"Robyn, you did what?"

"Dezzy, before I realized what I was doing I was in her face. I couldn't let her continue to disrespect Keisha's death. When I approached her she was alone. How was I supposed to know she wasn't by herself?"

"Robyn, have you lost your mind? You must not know who you're messing with! Those females are dangerous. They don't play."

"Yeah, well now it's too late. Those hoes are after me and I don't know what to do."

"Where are you now?"

"When the police saw the confusion, I was able to slip away. I'm in Richmond at Chevy's."

"Stay there, I'm on my way."

"Please hurry, Dezzy. They're closing in twenty minutes."

When I pulled into the Chevy's parking lot, it was empty with the exception of Robyn's Expedition which sat on a flat. I looked around several times for Robyn before getting out of my car to call her name. When I opened the car door, Robyn stepped out of the shadows on the side of the building and began rushing toward my car. She was less than ten feet away when a female appeared from the opposite side of Robyn's truck holding a .45. Seconds later, a Suburban raced up next to the truck as the female aimed the gun at Robyn's stomach. Robyn stood frozen in the headlights as the gun was cocked. In a split second, I dove in front of Robyn as the shot went off followed by screeching tires.

Chapter Six

I heard whispers in the distance but as my bladder became full, the voices were loud and clear. When I opened my eyes, the talking ceased all together.

"Dezzy, baby don't you ever scare me like that again."

My room was filled with roses and balloons were scattered here and there. The nurse came in to check my vitals and make sure all my needs were met. Even though I didn't like hospitals, Alta Bates in Berkeley always made me feel at home. My mother was stroking my head while my brother sat in a chair near the bed staring at me.

"Mom, I've got to pee."

She helped me out of the bed being careful not to touch my left shoulder — that's where I'd been shot. She attempted to come in the bathroom with me but soon surrendered after my insistence. I pulled the I.V. pole with my right hand and closed the door behind me. I could hear my mother whimpering again and my brother trying his best to console her. I took my time in the bathroom. I didn't want to face my mother and see her cry at my expense. It was eating me up inside. When she excused herself out of the room, I came out of the bathroom.

"Mama's still stressing but I know you're all right. I'm just ready to find the bitches that did this to you."

"Why, so you can be laying in the bed next to me?"

"I'm your brother, I'm supposed to protect you."

"Yeah, you're my brother and I want you around."

I noticed my blood-stained dress balled up in a plastic bag along with my purse. I didn't see any of my jewelry — I figured my mother had it. The bouquets seemed to be in competition, each one gorgeous offering something the next didn't.

"Where did all these flowers come from, Donte?"

"Well, you know word travels fast and as soon as five o'clock hits, they'll be back."

"Man, I never knew how much I was appreciated until now."

"Who's Diandre?"

"What?"

"You heard me. Camille and Blu brought that humongous bouquet and teddy bear right there from him."

My brother was referring to the three dozen red roses with baby's breath and mink teddy bear sitting at my side. An unopened card sat in the roses. The card wasn't within my reach so my brother handed it to me. Considering the circumstances, I'd already forgiven Diandre before I read the card:

I felt like a complete idiot when you walked out my door last night.
I overreacted and took it out on you, that's not right.
I guess I got jealous and didn't realize there was no need to be.
After all, you still came home with me.
I wanted to bring you the flowers myself but I didn't know
if you would have me after the way you left.
If you have an opportunity, please call me.
I would love to see you, touch you, and make you feel better.

I Love You,
Diandre

Love? Now was he laying it on thick or did he really feel this way? Love has many components. Though I've forgiven him, Diandre still needs to prove himself in the love category. I'll admit there is a special bond I feel to Diandre I haven't experienced before but I'm not sure it would be classified as love. It may be but I'm not ready to lower the guards of my heart and be vulnerable leaving myself open to hurt and pain.

"So when can I meet him?"

"Why, so you can run him off with your over-protective-big-brother tendencies?"

"Well, somebody has to screen the dudes you deal with."

"You'll meet him soon enough."

I was wrapping up my phone conversation with Diandre when my mother walked back into the room. Her face was very solemn and she avoided eye contact. I handed the receiver to my brother, adjusted myself on the bed, and focused my attention on my mother.

"Mama, what's wrong?"

"I just came back from visiting Robyn."

"She's here? I don't understand. I'm positive I pushed her out of the way."

"Yes, baby you did. After the sight of you being shot, she went into premature labor. The whole ordeal was too much to handle..."

"Mama, this story has holes in it. She's okay, right?"

"She's stable now. She went into convulsions and put extra strain on the twins..."

My mother's voice drifted off and tears began flowing, again. I didn't know what to expect based on my mother's actions. The numb feeling that came over my body suggested the pending news wasn't going to be pleasing. As much as I desired to know what was going on, I wasn't eager for sad news. I decided I'd let my mother pace herself and tell me in her own time.

"Dezzy, her little boy didn't make it."

A knot formed in the pit of my stomach followed by a lump in my throat. I wanted to believe I'd heard my mother incorrectly and all said was a huge misunderstanding but she said nothing more. My mother walked over to her bag and pulled out her Bible. She sat in a chair across the room. When my mother got ready to pray no one was to disturb her. She always told me and Donte prayer changes things and after the many things my small family had survived, I believed her. At times, though, I felt like she was the only one who knew how to get a prayer through. It often seemed my prayers failed to be answered. Time and time again, I would share this with my mother and without fail she assured me my prayers would be answered but on His time — I wasn't the one calling the shots. If at no other time, I would hope He'd hear my prayers now. A very close friend of mine was experiencing something devastating and I shared her pain. As much as I wanted to be there for her, I couldn't begin to figure out how.

I'd asked one of the nurses to connect me to her room. I didn't have much to say but I was more than willing to lend an ear and that's what I did. Other than Keisha's death, I'd never felt so helpless. When the subject matter began to be too much for her to bear, Trevell took the phone and politely concluded the conversation. I handed the receiver to my brother then lay in the bed with an incredible numbness. In a matter of moments, everything had changed drastically. If only it could all be done over...

Donte went home but my mother remained by my side until sunrise. When I woke up, she was stroking my head. Her eyes were bloodshot from crying all night and she looked worn out in general. I wanted her to go home and rest but she resisted, at least until I ate breakfast. The nurse came, checked my vitals, and two hours later brought me breakfast. My mother joined me and had coffee and a bagel. When she almost dropped her coffee because she was falling asleep, I told her to go home and continued to press the issue until she finally did. Besides, I hadn't had a moment to myself so I welcomed the opportunity.

After my mother left, I flipped through the channels until I landed on Ricki Lake. I was trying to take my mind off of all the happenings in my life. The nurse came in with my medication. Within twenty minutes, the pills had taken affect and I was struggling to stay awake. By the time Ricki went to commercial break, I was watching my eyelids.

I hadn't realized I'd slept the day away until I opened my eyes and peered out the window at the pink sky as the sun was setting. The nurse left a tray with dinner, but I wasn't feeling the mashed potatoes and roast beef — I didn't touch it. The news was too depressing but nothing else was on television. I watched about five minutes of the top story before finally turning it off. My brother bought Eric Jerome Dickey's, "*Liar's Game*" and left it for me. It wasn't long before I was completely immersed in the novel. I had been so wrapped up in chapter five I didn't notice the door open. I already knew who'd walked through the door without looking. The seducing smell of his cologne soon filled the room. I sat the book down and turned my attention to Diandre who continued to hold open the door as if someone were coming behind him.

"Judging by the icicles on your tray, you will appreciate this burrito I brought you."

"Mexicali Rose?"

"With enchilada sauce and cheese on top just how you like it."

"Thank you so much, baby." I gestured for him to come over.

"Just a second, Dezzy. I'm not alone."

"Diandre, who did you bring up here? You know I look a mess."

"Trust me, baby. He ain't trippin'.'"

As Diandre finished his sentence, an adorable two foot chocolate chip walked through the door barely able to hold his balance. Like his daddy, he wore dark denim jeans, blue and white Air Force Ones, with blue Phat Farm t-shirts. Diandre's son was a miniature version of him. Diandre closed the door behind his son as he stuck close by his daddy's side. Diandre pulled a chair by my bedside then handed me the foil wrapped Styrofoam. His son was in his lap moments later.

"Diandre, you know I'm not going to be able to finish all of this. You'll have to take it home for me so it won't go bad."

His son peered at me with big almond-shaped brown eyes. When I winked at him, he blushed and hid his face in his father's chest. Diandre looked at him and laughed.

"What's your name, handsome?"

"Kendrick." He continued to face his daddy.

"How old are you, Kendrick?"

"Two."

"Wow, you're an old man!"

"Nuh uh," he giggled.

"Dezzy, don't let him fool you. He's not shy. He's playing the role."

"Do you want some of my burrito, Kendrick?"

He shook his head then climbed off of his daddy to explore the small room. Diandre found a pen and paper for Kendrick, pulled an action figure out of his pocket and gave him everything along with a sucker. Once Kendrick was situated on the floor, Diandre returned to my side.

The nurse walked into the room, removed my tray, checked my vitals, gave me a final dosage of medication and informed me I would be discharged first thing in the morning. The news was pleasing but Diandre appeared to be much happier than I was. I was happy to be going home but I couldn't help thinking about Robyn. This was going to be a trying time for her and I wanted to be there for her by any means necessary. I only hoped I'd be able to.

"Where's your mind, baby? You haven't said anything else since you started eating."

"I'm just thinking, Diandre. Not to mention, I'm hungry so my conversation right this moment is very minimal."

"I see you got my flowers."

"Mmm hmm."

"Did you read my card?"

"Mmm hmm."

"Is all forgiven?"

"I guess."

"You guess?"

"I'm playing. You know I can't stay mad at you."

"On the real, Dezzy I apologize for coming at you the way I did."

"I know. Diandre let it go."

"You're special to me, Dezzy. I let you meet the number one priority in my life."

"Diandre, I was going to have to eventually in the event our relationship escalated any more."

"Well as you can see, there is no time like the present."

"Would you like to take me home in the morning?"

"Oh, I get to see your crib?"

"The temporary one... should you choose to take me home."

"You didn't have to fix your lips to ask me. I'll be here."

"Thanks, boo."

"Don't mention it. I love you, Dezzy."

The bite I'd taken went down hard. I knew he was waiting on my response but I couldn't bring myself to talk. Sure, I cared about Diandre a great deal but the last man I'd said those words to ended up scarring me pretty bad. I tried desperately not to carry baggage with me from my previous relationship but it was almost inevitable. Diandre stood next to my bed and looked down at me.

"Even though you haven't verbalized it, I know how you feel. Your actions towards me speak much louder than any word you could ever say."

I gazed into Diandre's eyes. He was right. There was no hiding my extreme fondness of him. Before I could muster a word, Diandre had already placed his warm lips on mine. I took his face in my right hand and exchanged myself with him the only way I could — given the circumstances. We pulled away slowly and Kendrick began snickering.

"Dezzy, let me get this little knucklehead home. I'll see you in the morning."

"Y'all be safe."

"We will. See you later."
"Bye Kendrick."
"Bye, bye."

I wrapped my burrito back up and handed it to Diandre. He took the burrito out of my hand, grabbed Kendrick off the floor then they were out the door as quickly as they'd come.

Before I fell asleep, I envisioned myself as a wife and mother. One part of me felt foolish for fantasizing about the future while the other part welcomed the opportunity. After all, the possibilities of the future are endless.

Chapter Seven

Diandre pulled next to my El Dorado in the driveway and was opening my door when a loud crashing sound came from within my house. I heard my brother yelling and with Diandre's help, I rushed through the front door. Ahead of me was Raijean on the couch with her face buried in her hands. A vase of flowers were broken at her feet and my brother was pacing back and forth. He hadn't noticed Diandre and I had walked through the door.

"How in the hell could you be fucking another nigga... my best friend, Raijean? What kind of a female are you?"

"Donte, a female who thought enough of you to tell you the truth."

"Raijean, miss me with the bullshit. If you thought that much of me, you wouldn't have fucked him."

Diandre stayed close to the door while I walked further into the battlefield. In most cases, I would have been embarrassed to have Diandre meet my brother under these circumstances but I was more concerned about my brother's well-being at the time. It's not often my brother loses his temper.

"What's going on?" I asked.

"You're brother is going crazy."

"Raijean, I know my brother. He would have to be motivated. What did you do?"

"Tell her Raijean. Tell her how you may not be carrying my baby."

Donte hit the wall and the floor vibrated. He would hit everything around him in the room but he would never hit a female and I ultimately respected my brother for that. He turned to look at Raijean with major hurt in his eyes. She didn't return his glare. He turned and noticed Diandre in the room for the first time. Diandre nodded a hello to Donte who looked at him long and hard before returning the gesture. Once he had, he walked out of the room.

Raijean searched my face for answers but she found nothing. I was dumbfounded by the entire situation. There was nothing I could

tell her that would help. She created
this bed and now she was going to
have to lie in it. For her sake, I
really hoped the baby was Donte's
because if not she could forget it.
On the other hand, she wasn't
deserving of him.

"Dezzy, I don't know what to do."

"Raijean, I think you better leave."

Judging by my tone, she knew not
to question the idea. She
mechanically collected her things,
including the broken vase on the
floor, and walked out the door. I
began picking up the remains of the
flowers when Diandre walked over.

"Baby, that's not your problem." He
pulled me by my right elbow.

"I know but–"

"Your brother will handle it. You
need to rest. You can't take on
everyone else's burdens as much as
you think you can."

"What are you getting at?"

"Nothing, Dezzy... it's just that your
shoulders are weighed down enough
with your own concerns – deal with
that first."

"You're right. I at least need to go
and check up on him, though."

"I'll be here on the couch when you
get back."

My brother was in the kitchen with a bottle of Belvedere in one hand and a shot glass in the other. My heart jumped into my throat at the sight. My brother had battled and conquered, so I thought, alcoholism. I'd caught him off guard but he didn't let that stop him.

"Donte, what are you doing?"

"Not now, Dezzy."

"Not now my ass... Donte, you were doing so well."

My words seemed to echo in the kitchen. He was silent, in fact, he didn't move. Moments later, he heaved the bottle into the wall and the shot glass went crashing to the floor.

"You cannot let her bring this out of you."

"Dezzy, I really love her and that unborn child."

"I know you do."

"I can't believe she would do this to me... and Michael, oh my God I better not see that nigga on the street or it's on."

"All right, D... calm down."

"Why? He deserves everything that's coming to him."

"I agree with you but you don't have to be the one to bring the wrath."

"That's probably what he wants me to do so he can have her to himself."

"Well, if you feel that way don't give him the satisfaction."

For the first time during this moment, my brother had finally heard me. He looked at me and then all of the glass on the floor. I was still trying to figure out his disposition when he began laughing.

"Okay, D now you're scaring me."

"I almost took a drink."

"That's not funny."

"Oh, but it is. I didn't let her get the best of me."

Like that, my brother had done a complete three-sixty. His demeanor changed and he began cleaning the kitchen. I inquired about his well-being once more before finally returning to Diandre. I felt better knowing my brother was thinking logically again.

"Is everything all right, Dezzy?"

"Everything's fine."

My mother walked through the front door. She looked rested and had returned to her normal self. She wrapped up a business call on her cell phone while she hung up her jacket. When the call was over, she turned the phone off and slipped it into her coat pocket.

"Hey, baby how do you feel?"

"Much better. Mama, this is my friend, Diandre. Diandre, this is my mother, Sonya."

Diandre gave me a brief, awkward look that would have gone unnoticed by the average person but I picked up on it. He stood and walked over to my mother.

"How're you doing, Mrs...."

"It's Miss and call me, Sonya. I'm not old. Are you the person in my parking spot?"

"Oh, I'm sorry. I can move."

"Don't worry about it, baby. Make sure you park on the street next time."

They shared a laugh then my mother noticed the puddle of flowers on her carpet. Before she could say anything, I threw my hands up and pointed towards the kitchen. I didn't need to say any more. She was on a mission to find Donte. In the meantime, I led Diandre to my bedroom so we could be alone. He sat in the chair at my desk after glancing around the room then stared at me. I kicked off my shoes and climbed onto my bed before acknowledging it.

"Am I missing something? Why are you staring at me?"

"What am I to you?"

"I don't understand."

"How do you feel about me?"

"You're my sweetheart."

"Am I?"

"Diandre, why don't you get to what it is you're trying to say?"

"Why'd you tell your mama I'm your friend?"

"Oh, that's what this is about."

"Yes, it is... and why are you afraid to admit you love me?"

"Whoa, where is all of this coming from?"

"Admit it."

"Diandre, I care about you a great deal–"

"But do you love me?"

"And as far as you being a friend, was I wrong for saying that?"

"Well, no but I thought I was more than a friend."

"Diandre, what could I have said that would have been more to your liking?"

"Mama, I'd like for you to meet my boyfriend, Diandre or this is my man–"

"Okay, okay. I apologize, sweetie. From here on out, I will put the label on you."

"I mean, think about it, Dezzy. Would you like to be introduced as this girl or a friend?"

"Point well taken, it won't happen again."

"And don't think I've forgotten about the love question. You're conveniently skating all around the subject. You aren't slick."

"Is that what you want to hear, baby?"

"Yes. You may think it's a bit soon for me to feel this way but I believe in destiny, do you?"

Of course I believed in destiny. I'd never given much thought to the idea Diandre may feel the same way. I always assumed females were the ones who recognized a special bond before a man ever would.

I turned to look at Diandre. He continued to stare me down with the hopes of getting me to open up. As the room steadily filled with uncomfortable silence, he stood and walked over to the bed. He sat at the foot of the bed and began to rub my feet. Diandre definitely knew how to work magic with his hands. If I didn't already have serious feelings for him, this was one way to change my mind.

"Dezzy, maybe you don't realize how I feel about you. In due time, I will prove myself and you will see how serious I am."

As soon as Diandre finished his sentence, Donte appeared in the doorway. Seeing Diandre, he started to turn around and leave but I commanded him to come in. Donte didn't step very far into the room, only far enough so I wouldn't complain.

"Diandre, this is my brother and best friend, Donte.   D, this is my boyfriend, Diandre."

"Hey, Donte how you doin'?"

My brother had a blank look on his face before snapping back into reality. He stepped forward to shake Diandre's hand.

"Shit, despite everything going on right now, I can't complain... dawg, you look really familiar. Do I know you from somewhere?"

Diandre shook his head then went back to rubbing my feet. I could see the wheels turning in Donte's head but I didn't press the issue. Donte handed me a package that had been delivered earlier, checked to see if I needed anything then left the room.

"I get that a lot. I guess I have one of those faces."

Diandre's cell phone began to ring. Women's intuition told me who was on the line before Diandre ever opened his mouth. He stood, excused himself, and walked into my bathroom. I felt his actions were a bit out of character since he'd never taken a call in private before but I was determined to remain calm. I would definitely address this once the opportunity presented itself.

I was getting comfortable on my bed when I saw Donte pass my door and peer inside again. I didn't understand maybe there was something in the air because they were both acting strange. I was going to ask Donte to come inside and let me know what was bothering him when my mother informed him Raijean was on the phone. His entire demeanor changed. I wasn't going to attempt to talk to him now.

Five minutes of channel surfing passed before Diandre came out of the bathroom. He rushed over, gave me a quick peck on the lips and gave a lousy excuse for having to leave suddenly to attend to Kendrick. Being that he'd made reference to his son, I didn't question it. He did appear to be frustrated by what ever had just taken place – we'd talk later. I started to walk him to the door, but he assured me he could see his way out. He wanted me to get as much rest as possible. I didn't object. I was happy to be home in my own bed and I intended to take advantage of it.

After Diandre left, I closed and locked the door. It was nice to be back in my own private space without having interruptions every time I turned around. I'm thankful to be able to complain, though. There are many people I've known who haven't been as fortunate. With that thought, I relished in the fact I was alive. In fact, I was so grateful I did what I probably should do more often – I prayed. I was given another chance at life, now it was time to evaluate it. Today was the first day towards a new beginning.

Chapter Eight

Like always, business was booming because of the holidays. I was working twice as hard because I wouldn't be back in the shop until after the New Year. I'd already broken tradition and had clients come in on Christmas Eve but I figured it was the least I could do. I had three heads left before going home to prepare for Blu's record release party. Robyn was my last customer and she helped prep the others so we could leave on time.

I was proud of my friend. Amongst all the turmoil, she'd managed to overcome. Samarai, her daughter, was healthy and maturing quicker than ever. Her relationship with Trevell was rock solid and both were eager for their wedding day next month. In the meantime, I'd became Samarai's God Mother and attempted to assist Robyn in any way I could –

she still had rough days and when she did, I was there.

I was flat-ironing a client's hair when Lee walked through the door. She was going to the release party too but her hair opposed her plans. Before she could say anything, I knew what she wanted. As much as I could ring her neck for the last minute change, I loved my God Sister too much to leave her hanging. She knew this which is why she was at the bowl allowing Robyn to prepare her for a shampoo before I could comply. She and Robyn fell into a conversation quickly, and before long I'd finished two clients.

"Lee, could you do me a favor and lock the front door? I don't want anyone else trying to sneak in here last minute."

After shooting a don't go there look my way, she locked the door. Robyn changed the music from India Arie to a more upbeat Missy Elliot. Her excuse was to get us in a pre-party mood. I didn't argue because after the long day I'd had, I needed a pick-me-up. Robyn was wearing a straight, blunt look which took no time. Lee was wearing the more complicated straw-set. While Lee sat under the dryer, I gave myself the Farah Faucet flip 'do. We were all forty five minutes behind schedule but once we were dressed and ready to go the delay was well worth it.

Parking was scarce and the sidewalks congested in front of the Oakland Marriot. Fortunately, Diandre arranged for us to have a limousine drop us off to avoid chaos. In addition, our names were on the guest list so we bypassed the line. Inside, people mingled in separate circles. It was evident who was part of the upper echelon and who tried to appear to be. I was happy to be with my girls since all the bodies made it hard to recognize people I knew.

A server appeared to take our drink orders. I noticed a vacant table and informed the server where she could find us when she returned. We sauntered over to the table and gracefully took our seats. While we waited, we held conversation and casually people watched. We were running behind schedule but had arrived in enough time for Blu to come out, Camille on his arm, to say a few words. I listened to him speak while observing the people paying attention. Some women watched with admiration while others tried to kill Camille with their looks, eager to take her place. My cousin knew many women envied the role she played in Blu's life but she wasn't the least bit fazed. She knew what she had and how he felt about her. Before Blu returned the party to normal, he requested the presence of his right hand man, Diandre. He wanted everyone to know without the help of his producer, much of his success would be non-existent. This was the first time I would learn Diandre also served as Blu's manager.

I thought it strange Diandre was not around during such a special time. I tried to stay calm and not assume the worst. As if having deja vous, Lee tapped me on my shoulder and pointed out Diandre who was outside having a heated argument with a woman. Her back was to me so I had difficulties making out her face. When she finally turned around, trailing Diandre's heals, I made no mistakes figuring out the persistent woman was Justine. She attempted to put her arm through Diandre's but he was too quick. His pace quickened and his game face was in tact once he rejoined the party. My eyes met hers in no time. She appeared embarrassed but soon regained her composure and gave me a sneaky grin. The entire vibe changed once she stepped foot in the room.

"D, who's the hoe trying to swoop on your man?" Lee asked

"A hoe not worth the time."

"Well, the bitch is about to demand some time," Robyn stated. "She's on her way over here."

I looked up and sure enough this woman was approaching our table. I didn't understand her intentions but I would be ready nonetheless. I really hoped she wouldn't try and cause a scene. She walked slowly and strategically in my direction. I had a million things running through my mind but I knew I would not let this woman be the reason I established a record for myself tonight. Lee quickly slipped off her shoes, crossed her legs, and straightened the rings on her fingers, welcoming the challenge. Robyn had the same mindset. She pushed her chair away from the table making it easier for her to stand. I took a sip of my White Zinfandel and told both of them that wouldn't be necessary. When they were about to object, Justine was already at the table.

"Nice party, isn't it?"

I stared at her long and hard. She noticed the fourth empty seat and started towards it. Lee propped her feet up on the chair stopping her in the process.

"Oh, I can't join you ladies?"

"No." Robyn responded.

"Why are you hear, Justine? What do you want?"

"Oh, you know my name? Unfortunately, I can't say the same. Diandre has never mentioned yours."

She was trying to push my buttons. It was obvious. I wouldn't let her have the satisfaction. My East Oakland roots wanted to come out and give her a run for her money but my mother's upbringing quickly squashed the thought. As much as we all made it evident her presence was not wanted, she didn't budge. She continued to stand there and relish in her aggravation.

"Is there a reason you're still standing here?" I asked

"How long have the two of you been dating?"

"Long enough."

"Enough for what?"

Diandre appeared out of no where. He acknowledged Lee and Robyn, and tracked down a server. He requested five glasses of Cristal and occupied the fourth seat Lee offered him. Justine seemed aggravated she was still standing but pleased with the idea she was finally being included. People approached the table with demos and questions, Diandre politely turned them away. Diandre pulled me by my arm attempting to get me to stand. I did and Justine was in my seat in no time. I started to say something but Diandre pulled me into his lap before I had an opportunity. He gave my thigh a squeeze, pressed his lips softly against my cheek then went about normal conversation as if the moment were the least bit awkward. Following his lead, I decided to enjoy the company of my friends as if Justine weren't sitting there. I could have won an Emmy for my performance.

Robyn was yelling over the music wrapping up her phone call with Trevell when our glasses arrived. Justine reached into the table immediately and grabbed a glass before any of us had an opportunity to. Lee was about to open her mouth when Diandre spoke first.

"Justine, I'm glad you're eager to take part in the celebration."

The rest of us picked up our glasses while we listened to Diandre. I had to admit, the suspense was killing me.

"And what will we be celebrating, Diandre?" she asked.

She was purposely flirting with Diandre. I began stroking the back of his head. She shut up.

"Well, no matter how many times I've tried to prove myself or let it be known how determined I am to have my way or get others to see things my way... no one has made it more difficult than Dezzy. She questions my intentions on everything and always has something to say."

"What kind of woman would I be if I didn't?" I laughed.

"That's exactly my point. Believe it or not, Justine has helped open my eyes to what a real woman is... by being everything a real woman is not."

Lee and Robyn both laughed while I struggled to hold my composure. I wasn't sure where Diandre was going with this but I was eager to find out. Justine cleared her throat and tried to hide her embarrassment while Diandre continued talking.

"I know Dezzy is getting impatient and wants to know where this little speech is going."

All of our eyes were locked on Diandre. I had a million things running through my mind as to what he was trying to say but I held my tongue to ensure I wouldn't get ahead of myself and say the wrong thing.

"You know what, I've said all I have to say."

We all looked at each other with confusion on our faces. From the looks of things, Diandre had said a whole lot of nothing. As if responding to our puzzled looks, he reached in his pocket and sat a small black box on the table in front of me. I immediately grasped my chest while Justine rolled her eyes in disgust. I stared at the box trying to assure myself what I was seeing was a reality. I guess I stared too long because Lee picked up the box and opened it for me. Inside was a two-carat platinum diamond ring. I struggled to catch my breath while Diandre looked on with admiration.

"Dezzy, I think you know what I am trying to say."

"Flatter me baby, let me hear it."

"Dezzy, do me the honor and be my wife."

"Well, since you put it so eloquently, how can I resist?"

I extended my hand as Diandre picked up the ring. He slid it onto my finger as Lee and Robyn squealed in delight. For a brief moment, all people and sounds were blocked out of my mind. There was only me and Diandre gazing into one another's eyes validating the future we would share together. As the atmosphere faded its way back into my thought, I pressed my lips against his. Justine stood up so fast from the table, the chair fell to the floor. She rushed from the table and out the main door in the blink of an eye. My girls, being the females they are, applauded at her exit. Soon after, two gentlemen asked them to dance and they were lost in the mix.

"Now do you believe I love you?"

"Well, if you don't you sure do know how to fake it."

"How soon can you move in?"

"Whoa, baby. We haven't even been engaged an hour and you want me to move in with you?"

"Well, why not? I'm already more than prepared."

"Diandre, I need some time to think this through."

"I don't mean to put pressure on you, Dezzy. I'm only looking forward to us spending the rest of our lives together."

"Well, that makes two of us."

I kissed Diandre again making sure I didn't get too carried away. I had one mind to leave the party at that moment – that would be rude. As though Diandre was reading my mind, he whispered the thought in my ear. We quickly came to a mutual understanding – the party would have an hour more of our time before I politely explained to my girls the limousine would see them both home safely. In the meantime, Diandre and I would partake in Blu's success until we departed to have a celebration of our own.

It was easy to lose track of time once absorbed into the atmosphere. I hadn't had this much fun in a long time. Guests were dancing, participating in karaoke, mingling, sipping, or taking an occasional break for a bite to eat. One could conclude everyone was having a great time. Within this one moment, it seemed as though nothing could go wrong.

I'd found an empty seat to occupy and catch my breath while I watched others interact. Before I could get comfortable, my cell phone began to vibrate in my purse. My mother was out of town on business, my brother knew where I was and anyone else who would be calling me at this hour was in the room with me. I fumbled through my purse trying to retrieve my phone. Once I finally did, a text message appeared demanding I call Katryna on her cell phone right away. As much as I wanted to avoid the call, I soon found myself slipping through the crowd into the bathroom to return the call.

The bathroom was surprisingly empty when I walked inside. I was fortunate since the only other quiet place was outside the party all together. I began dialing the number Katryna left in my phone.

"What's up Katryna?"

"Dezzy, are you okay? Is Robyn all right?"

"I'm fine, she's cool. Why what's up?"

"Every since you took the bullet for Robyn, they've been looking for her."

"How did you know about me getting shot, Katryna?"

"You told me."

"That's bullshit, Katryna and you know it. I haven't talked to you since we were at Robyn's house." My voice drifted because everything was happening fast and was too eerie to imagine.

Katryna was silent as commotion began to stir on her end. It became evident she was sneaking to speak on the telephone. I didn't recognize any of the voices in the background but several females could be heard from a distance.

"Katryna, are you in trouble?"

"I can't talk." She whispered.

"What's going on Katryna? Where are you?"

A female's voice became prominent in the background as Katryna quickly mumbled her whereabouts into the phone.

"Dezzy, please... do whatever you have to do. I need you to come and get me or I'm dead."

The anonymous voice was now in the same room as Katryna. She spoke with force making the average person feel easily intimidated. She shouted obscenities at Katryna then the line went dead.

I was beginning to feel as though my loyalty to people I cared about was being tested. Sure, God wouldn't give me any more than I could handle but even He seemed to be stretching my patience thin. Needless to say, if the tables were turned I would want someone to do the same for me. I had no idea what awaited me but unlike my encounter with Robyn, I would be prepared.

I quickly jotted down the address Katryna had given on a napkin before it had an opportunity to slip my mind. I put my phone on my body in case she had a chance to call again then I went to round up help. This time, I wasn't going down without a fight.

Chapter Nine

Despite our initial plans for the evening, Diandre and I were joined by Lee and two of his down-for-my-niggas type friends. They were two rough dudes who made their careers as criminals. I questioned how Diandre came to get involved with them but dismissed it as "peoples" everyone has when dirty work needs to be done but certain hands remain clean. We were in an unmarked van outside of Katryna's hostage space. Had anyone asked me three hours prior, I never would have said I'd be celebrating my engagement with two strangers at two o'clock in the morning on a semi-deserted street in Pinole.

Seeing as how I'd never broken into anywhere, I was relying on MacGuyver and Nino Brown to initiate the move. In the meantime, Lee and I sat on edge in the back of the van watching the two experts prepare for what appeared to be a miniature war. Diandre sat low in the driver's seat keeping an eye on the house. In hushed tones, he informed us three females had left, two bodies could still be seen moving around in the living room, and the remainder of the house was dark. The criminals, who remained nameless, said it was almost show time. Apparently, they both knew about the female gang who occupied this house. They explained to us these girls had no remorse for life and thrived off the misery of others. As much as they were supposed to serve as family to one another, they believed everyone was disposable if necessary. The rudest awakening I received was learning only members stepped foot into the home. This information meant one thing, and if it weren't for the fact she had no one else to turn to, I would have left Katryna there.

The professionals zipped up their black leather coats and handed me a black pull over. One of them lowered a black ski mask on his face while the other handed me a small black .38. I'd never used a gun before and hoped I wouldn't start now. I didn't want to go inside but I was the only one who'd be able to identify Katryna. Before I touched the gun, Lee handed me the gloves sitting next to me. I have never been more nervous in my life. She'd come along for moral support and in case her assistance was needed once Katryna was with us. Considering the circumstances, should she be hurt, we couldn't exactly take Katryna to the emergency room.

Diandre announced the living room light had been turned off. Now there was only the glow of the television seeping through the cracks of the blinds. He saw the fear in my face and assured me his friends wouldn't let anything happen to me. I prayed Diandre was right. I'd been given a second chance at life and I didn't want to blow it now. Lee said a silent prayer as we filed out the back of the van.

The gun was tucked behind me in my waistband should I need it. The plan was to have me knock on the door while one of the guys went around the back. The other would stand close by me on the porch but out of sight. Once the door was opened, he would attack if necessary.

113

My knees were wobbling as I climbed the stairs. Nino Brown was right by my side. When he took his position, I swallowed hard and proceeded to knock on the door. The television was loud on the other side of the door so I tried the doorbell. The noise subsided as footsteps were heard approaching the door.

The door swung open without warning. In front of me stood a young girl with an aged face. I assumed she'd had a hard upbringing. She stared at me briefly before acknowledging me.

"What do you want?"

"I'm here for Katryna."

"And who are you supposed to be?"

"Is she here?"

"Yeah."

"Can I see her?"

"No."

The girl shifted her weight from one foot to the other. In doing so, she cleared enough space for me to see Katryna slumped over and strapped to a chair. I wasn't clear if the sudden view was deliberate but in that moment all the stakes had been raised. She attempted to close the door in my face when I put my foot in the doorway.

"Bitch, are you crazy?"

"I'm not leaving without my cousin."

I could see MacGuyver had made his way inside. He noticed Katryna but bypassed her to locate the other female in the house. I kept my eyes on the girl at the door so she wouldn't become suspicious. Seeing I wasn't going to let up, her face became violent and she stepped towards me. I panicked inside but my face never cracked. When she reached towards her waist I shot a glance at Nino who appeared out of no where and caught her off guard. He aimed a .45 directly at her face, she backed up. I ran past the both of them and directly over to Katryna. I untied her in records time but because she was out cold she couldn't help me get her out the door. I began smacking her face as commotion stirred in the back of the house. She whimpered slightly but wasn't as conscious as I would have liked. I put her arm around my shoulders as a shot rang out in the back of the house. It wasn't long before I was making a move towards the door, dragging Katryna by my side. As we reached the front door, Nino explained we didn't have much time. I was to get Katryna to the van while he and MacGuyver tied up loose ends before the other females returned. We stumbled down the steps and Katryna fell in the street. Lee opened the back doors of the van and I dragged Katryna the rest of the way.

Once inside the van, Lee retrieved her first aid kit and began attempts at reviving Katryna. Diandre started the van and more shots were heard. I muffled my screams as the van began coasting. In a split second, the professionals hopped in and closed the doors. As Diandre sped away, I prayed these troubles were finally over. I didn't know what had taken place inside the house and I didn't want to. The less I knew the better. I only wanted to get as far away as possible and forget any of this ever happened.

Diandre drove the van back to the Berkeley Marina where our cars were parked. I thanked his friends and climbed out of the van. Katryna moved slowly but she was doing better. She sat in the backseat of my car. Lee stayed by her side. Despite their differences, Lee knew her priorities. She would do what was necessary to help. I gave Diandre a hug and kiss on the cheek then left him with his friends to finalize their business. I slid behind my wheel and drove home.

Katryna lay across my bed while I inflated the air mattress. We'd been alone for fifteen minutes now. Lee suggested she lay low for a while until it seemed safe to go to the hospital for a more thorough examination. On the outside, she suffered scratches and bruises but Lee questioned whether or not she had a cracked rib. She had given Katryna Tylenol and Motrin then left. I was still shaken but figured the worst was over.

I grabbed a pair of pajamas for myself and handed another to Katryna. She changed slowly and climbed into my bed. I was wired and had several thoughts running through my mind at the moment. I put on my pajamas and collapsed onto the air mattress. We both laid in silence for about ten minutes. When the silence became too much for me to bear, I sat up and demanded Katryna's attention. I startled her because she'd already fallen asleep.

"How long have you been a member?"

She adjusted herself into a sitting position and looked at me.

"Three years."

I was overcome with anger when my heart fluttered. It had never crossed my mind before now. Three years was more than enough time to be aware of Keisha's murder. I turned to look at Katryna but she avoided my eyes.

"You knew they were going to kill Keisha, didn't you?

Katryna was silent then dropped her head. Even though she'd said nothing, she answered the question. I found myself struggling to breathe. She spoke several apologies at me but I wasn't receptive. I'd help save her life and she'd had a hand in taking the life of one of my closest friends. I couldn't mutter another word. I went into my bathroom to have some water. When I returned, she knew better than to speak to me. I turned off the lights and laid on the air mattress in complete darkness. I would need God's guidance to forgive her but this was a fact of life I would never forget.

Katryna had no problems falling asleep. The only explanation I could find was her being used to this lifestyle. While she enjoyed a long, hard slumber, I cried myself to sleep wishing I could somehow turn back the hands of time. I also made a promise to myself to end my relationship with Katryna once her health returned. If I continued to associate with her, I would be just as reliable for Keisha's death. I refused to be a hypocrite.

Chapter Ten

The fiasco from the night before was on the front page of the Oakland Tribune. I was in the kitchen with my mother while she prepared breakfast so I didn't want to give myself away by reacting too soon. One of the females had been pronounced dead at the scene while the other fought for her life in Highland Hospital. Fortunately, the Pinole Police Department had no leads. The headline read: *The Perfect Homicide?* I felt better knowing there were no suspects but my excitement soon changed to regret. A young woman was dead, another fighting for her life and I knew why. I tried not to be too hard on myself and passed it off as due justice.

My mother sat a platter of pancakes in front of me followed by a big bowl of scrambled eggs with cheese, a tray of bacon, and a bowl of fresh fruit. She knew Katryna was here. Every since Donte and I were younger, when we had company she'd blow the dust off of the pots and pans. I didn't tell my mother the details surrounding Katryna's sudden visit and when she saw her, I hoped she wouldn't ask too many questions. She ran some water in the skillet she'd scrambled the eggs then placed it on the stove above a small flame. She'd turned me and my brother on to that trick early on to make cleaning easier. After she placed four plates on the table, she sat down across from me.

"So when are you going to explain the rock that's blinding me on your finger?"

I'd been so concerned with other issues, I'd forgotten to mention my big news to my mother. Before I could go into the details of the story, she picked up my left hand and examined the ring more closely. After practically disconnecting my wrist, she sat my hand down and looked at me once again.

"So the roughneck knows how to pick 'em, huh?"

"Yeah, he didn't do too bad."

"I know I'm gone a lot but when did all of this happen?"

"Mom, I haven't been hiding anything. He asked me last night."

"You don't think this is a bit soon?"

"Mama, we've been dating for over six months and we're only engaged. It's not like I'm getting married tomorrow. People have long engagements all of the time."

"What ever happened to requesting permission to have my daughter's hand in marriage?"

"Mama, my daddy's dead–"

"And I became both your mama and your daddy."

"Don't you trust I can make the right decision?"

"Dezzy, I know you're grown baby. I just want you to be careful."

"I will... he wants me to move in with him. What should I do?"

"Why are you asking me? You're grown, remember?"

She gave a sly grin and stood up from the table. Donte and Katryna filed into the kitchen like elementary school kids would the cafeteria. It wasn't long before we were all stuffing our faces. Donte attempted to ask Katryna about her appearance but I kicked him before he could complete the sentence – he'd caught my drift. Between bites, Katryna informed us she'd be returning to her apartment today before catching a flight to Los Angeles. She was going to move in with her aunt. I silently wished her well and prayed she'd begin a new, more positive life for herself. Donte agreed to see her home and make sure she made it to the airport.

Several hours later, I had the house to myself. Donte was at Raijean's — they'd worked out their differences — and my mother was spending the night with her new honey. I was having a Calgon bath when my cell phone rang. I hesitated at first because the phone was on my bed and though it was only a few feet away, it seemed like miles. I bypassed my towel and ran straight over to the bed.

"Hey, baby you busy?"

"Soaking in the tub and thinking about you."

"Why didn't you call?"

"I was going to call you. Merry Christmas... I bought you a gift."

"Oh, you're going to spoil me too?"

"Don't get used to it."

"Whatever, Dezzy. Can I come get it?"

"The present isn't going anywhere. You can come and get *it* though."

"Anyone home?"

"Nope... nothing but space and opportunity here."

"Get out the tub and skip the towel. I'm on my way."

Diandre arrived an hour later. He walked through the door carrying gifts. I was taken aback. I was under the impression the ring on my finger was my gift. He sat the gifts on the coffee table then took off his jacket and hung it by the door. When I looked at the boxes more closely, one was for my mother! He was really attempting to earn brownie points now.

"Diandre, what's all this?"

"I got your mother a desk clock for her office and the other two are for you."

"What is it?"

"Open it and see!"

One of the boxes contained a gold and silver Anne Klein watch. The other was empty. When I turned my attention back to Diandre, he'd already began unfastening his pants. I grabbed both boxes and led Diandre to my bedroom. I intended to make Christmas very Merry.

Once we were in my bedroom, I pulled the covers back on my bed and climbed inside. Diandre shut my bedroom door, locked it and turned out the light. My room was completely black. I couldn't see my hand if I held it in front of my face. Diandre purposely made noise around the room so I wouldn't know which way he'd come from. For a brief moment, there was no movement at all. Suddenly, the covers were raised at my feet as he dived under. I let out a shriek as he began tickling and kissing me under the covers. Diandre enjoyed teasing me and he did so until I begged for his love.

After our bodies became one, I lost track of time. He and I both performed as if it were the last time we would. Perhaps the burst of energy came from our delayed lovemaking. Needless to say, we were making up for lost time. We loved the entire night through. When we finally decided to rest, the sun was beginning to rise. I laid my head on his chest, our legs were intertwined, and I smiled on the inside as I enjoyed the best feeling in the world.

When I woke up later that morning, it was eleven o'clock and Diandre was still sleeping. I slipped out of bed and into the shower. I had to meet Lee and Robyn to have the final bridal gown fitting. With Diandre sleeping, I was able to get more accomplished. I hated to wake him but now I was ready to leave. I tried to wake him with a soft kiss on his lips. When that didn't work, I caressed his member – his eyes shot open.

"Hey, babe... why are you dressed all ready?"

"I have to meet Lee and Robyn for the final gown fitting."

"Well, I thought we'd spend some time together."

"Diandre, you can have me to yourself later."

"Damn, don't you get tired of seeing them?"

"No. Why are you acting like this?"

"Shit, Dezzy I want to spend time with you."

"And I said we would later."

"I don't want to later. I want to spend time with you now. Why do you always have to put those hoes ahead of me?"

"Excuse me?"

"Look, Dezzy I didn't mean that."

"Hoes?"

"Dezzy, I'm sorry."

"Is that how you really feel about them?"

"No, Dezzy look–"

"Can you please leave?" I was calm.

"Dezzy–"

"No, as a matter of fact, I'll go. Please don't be here when I get back." My voice cracked but I refused to release tears.

Diandre had really hurt me. He knew my circle of friends was small and those I considered friends were close to me. Even if he felt they weren't important, he didn't need to verbalize it in front of me. I opened my bedroom door and slammed it behind me.

We'd finished the final fitting at two-thirty. It was now five o'clock. I was purposely dragging out the time since Diandre had pissed me off. He'd been repeatedly calling my cell phone but I avoided his calls. I would eventually talk to him but it would be on my own time. In the meantime, I'd gone splurging with my girls.

We were having dinner at the Olive Garden when Robyn took a call from

Trevell.   Watching the way she interacted on the phone made me realize how much I missed Diandre. Sure, I was upset he'd called them out their names but I felt he'd received the silent treatment long enough. He answered the phone on the first ring.   I listened to his numerous apologies as well as his promise to never talk about anyone close to me again. I took his words at face value and forgave him. After I ended my call, we paid the bill and went our separate ways. I returned home, grabbed some clothes and went to Diandre's house. I intended to keep the promise I'd made earlier with regards to us spending time with one another that evening.

"I already have a key for you, Dezzy. Wouldn't it be a lot easier for you to move in?   All of your belongings would already be here."

"Why do you want me here so bad?"

"Well, correct me if I'm wrong but I was under the impression married couples live together."

"You're right but we're not married."

"We will be. I've already shown you I'm not bullshitting."

"Okay."

"Okay? What do you mean okay?"

"I'll move in."

"Great, when?"

Diandre had a look about him I'd never seen before. It was a type of excitement I wasn't used to. He picked me up by my waist and spun me around. I was extremely dizzy when my feet landed on the floor but I managed to let him know I'd begin packing my things the next day. Diandre appeared satisfied. After a night of continuous talking, we finally decided to turn in. I would need plenty of rest to prepare for tomorrow.

My phone was off while I was at Diandre's house, so I wasn't aware I had messages until I turned my phone on once I was in my car. I was stopped at a red light while I listened to the messages. The first message was marked urgent and came from Donte. He'd never marked a message urgent, so I was concerned. I called him back before I listened to the rest of the messages.

"What's wrong Donte?"

"Dezzy, come home right now. We need to talk."

"I'm on my way right now. What's wrong? Is something wrong with mama?"

"No, just come home right now."

"Okay, okay. I'm on my way."

I burned up the freeway getting home. I pulled into my driveway in records time. Where my mother's car would normally be parked rested Donte's father's car. As I fumbled for my keys, Mr. Sutter opened the door.

"Hello, Desrinique how are you?"

"I'm pretty good, and you?"

I was nervous. Donte's father was a detective. It wasn't often he came around. I wondered about his sudden visit. I hoped new evidence hadn't been found regarding the homicide. I decided I wasn't going to say anything unless he did. I tried to act normal as I walked past him into the living room.

"Donte what was so pressing?"

"D, I don't really know how to tell you this."

"Spare me the small talk and say it, please."

"Dezzy..."

"Damnit, Donte tell me!"

"D, you've got to watch your back."

"I always do. Where is all of this coming from? You're scaring me, Donte."

"My dad is still looking into it for me... let's just say your boy Diandre isn't the perfect guy you think he is."

"What are you talking about?"

"Well, do you remember I thought he looked familiar? My father and I have been doing some research and we found out–"

"Donte, I don't want to hear this shit! What is this nonsense you're telling me? Who gave you permission to start researching my life?"

"Damnit, Dezzy don't be so damn stubborn. Why don't you hear what we have to say? Has he begun to flash on you yet?"

I didn't respond. While Diandre had tripped out on me on more than one occasion, I didn't think much of it. Every couple has their arguments. He and I aren't supposed to agree on everything. I decided I'd keep my mouth shut as opposed to entertain their ludicrous accusations any further.

"Desrinique, I have reason to believe this man may be dangerous."

"I've heard enough."

"Just be careful, Dezzy."

I walked to my room without muttering another word. I was furious. I was upset Donte went to his father before coming to speak with me and equally upset they would take my personal life into their hands. When will people finally treat me as the adult I am rather than a child! Granted, their intentions may be good, neither of them provided me with any solid proof to support their claims. Besides, I'd met Diandre through my very own cousin. She'd never intentionally introduce me to a man who was no good for me. If anyone could provide answers she could. I picked up my cordless phone and began dialing her number immediately.

"Hey, Camille how's it going, girl?"

"I just closed the deal on a home I've been trying to sell for the last four months!"

"Congratulations... do you have a minute?"

"Always, cousin... what's the matter?"

"Nothing really. How long did you know Diandre before introducing us?"

"About a month, why?"

"A month? I was under the impression you'd known him for quite some time."

"Well, not exactly. Blu knows other artists he manages and produces. He was unhappy with his previous representation so a friend referred Diandre. He and Blu did most of their communicating over the phone until they finally met a month before I introduced you."

I listened intently. I soon realized Camille wasn't as familiar with Diandre as I'd expected her to be. From what I was gathering, she didn't know Diandre well at all and what Blu knew was mainly business related. I continued to stay calm. I didn't want to jump to conclusions that could embarrass us all but for what it was worth, I'd keep a mental note of what everyone mentioned.

Camille and I talked for twenty minutes. I intentionally held her on the phone and held mini conversations to appear as though my main reason for calling was not solely Diandre. Once the call ended, I bean sorting through my things while I self-reflected. I only hoped Donte and his father were wrong. I waited a long time for Diandre – he was my first breath of fresh air in a long time.

Chapter Eleven

Several weeks later I was all moved in to my home in Fremont. Robyn's beautiful wedding had come and gone. Now, I could think about planning my own. My mother's opinion with this matter meant the world to me so I would begin planning once she returned from her conference in Washington, D.C. In the meantime, I dog-eared pages within different magazines with ideas I had. I was researching catering companies over the internet when I was interrupted by the doorbell. Robyn stood on the other side of the door holding Samarai on one hip with the diaper bag on the other.

"Please take this child. She is working my last nerve!"

Samarai was going to stay the night so Robyn and Trevell could have the evening to themselves. I looked forward to our time together. Samarai was my child once removed.

I spent time with her when ever I could but the best part was always giving her back at the end of the day. Samarai jumped into my arms and Robyn was gone in the blink of an eye.

Samarai and I enjoyed a peanut butter and jelly sandwich before I put her down for an afternoon nap. I knew I'd have at least two hours to get any unfinished business handled. I did two loads of laundry, restored the kitchen and put on dinner all before five o'clock. Diandre would be returning from a day with Kendrick any moment. I wanted to be able to relax once they did. Thirty minutes later, I was tackled by a very hyper Kendrick.

"Hi, Dezzy! Daddy's going to get me a snake like the one at the zoo."

"Oh, no daddy isn't!"

Kendrick looked at his father who shrugged his shoulders. His spirits appeared broken so I reassured him he would get something to have as a pet, not a snake though. He liked the idea of having something as opposed to nothing at all. I gave him a kiss on the forehead and instructed him to wash up for dinner. Diandre was told the same – he went upstairs and changed his clothes all together. I was preparing their plates when Diandre appeared next to me out of nowhere.

"What the fuck is Samarai doing here?"

I sat the plate on the table and looked at Diandre as though he'd lost his mind. His outbursts were happening far too frequent. I wasn't going to tolerate much more.

"What's the problem, Diandre? She comes over all the time."

"That's exactly my point. You didn't ask me if she could come over."

He was treating me as though I were a child. This was the second time he acted like I needed his permission before doing something. I was about to let Diandre have it when Kendrick ran into the kitchen. I didn't like to argue in front of children. I poured Kendrick a cup of apple juice and sat it next to his plate. Once he was all squared away, I left the kitchen to attend to a crying Samarai.

I stayed in the guest room with Samarai that night. Despite all of his attempts to make it better, he was going to learn he couldn't talk to me any kind of way. While lying next to Samarai, I decided ignoring him wouldn't be enough. I would teach him a lesson by giving him some space. Space would allow me time to clear my head and hopefully provide Diandre with an opportunity to get his shit together. I slept well feeling I'd found a feasible solution to our problems.

Robyn was gardening in her yard when I pulled up. I left my car running while I unloaded Samarai and her belongings. Robyn realized this wouldn't be a long visit so she helped me speed everything along. She inquired about the perplexed look on my face. I gave her an answer brief enough to satisfy her concerns while still holding on to my privacy. I didn't feel like doing a lot of explaining. I assured her I'd call later then headed to my God sister's house. She never failed to be there for me when I was having male issues.

"Lee, I don't know why Diandre has been flashing so much lately."

"Have you thought about hearing what your brother has to say?"

"To be honest, I'm still upset with Donte. I love my brother to death but I feel like he went behind my back."

"Dezzy, I think you need to get over it and hear him out."

"Maybe."

"Well, feel free to stay as long as you'd like, okay?"

"Thanks, I really appreciate it-"

"I know you would do the same for me so don't worry about it."

She was right. If the tables were turned I wouldn't think twice about reaching out to her. I only prayed she was never in my situation.

"I ordered Chinese food right before you got here. The man should be here in another twenty minutes. I hope you're hungry."

"Famished. I was so upset I skipped dinner and was so busy earlier I didn't have time for breakfast or lunch."

Lee ironed her uniforms for the week while I rescheduled my appointments for the next two days. I sat some money on the table for Lee and headed for the bathroom as the doorbell rang. My mouth was already salivating for the food. I'd just flushed the toilet when I heard muffled arguing from the living room.

When I opened the bathroom door, I could hear Diandre yelling.

"Where's Dezzy?"

"Why?"

"Don't ask questions. Where is she?"

"Wait a minute, who in the hell do you think you are?"

"Lee, I don't have the time. Where is she?"

"She isn't here."

"Why are you lying? Her car is parked up the street."

Lee held the door with one hand forcing Diandre to stand outside. It never crossed my mind Diandre would actually come looking for me. I knew Diandre wouldn't back down until he spoke with me so I walked up behind Lee at the door. She looked at me as though I weren't making the right decision but backed away. Diandre looked disheveled and his eyes were vacant.

"Let's go."

"I'm not going anywhere."

"I said let's go."

"And I said no!"

"Who in the fuck are you yelling at?"

Now I was convinced Diandre had lost his mind. His eyes filled with hatred as my brother's words began to run through my head. I stared at

him.   He was completely silent in
return. I repeated myself quietly but
firm,   "Diandre, I   am   not   going
anywhere."

Diandre had selective hearing. He
grabbed me by my arm and yelled,
"Yes you are!"

"Let me go."

"What?"

"Let me go!"

The delivery man looked frightened
as he walked up to the door behind
Diandre.   Ignoring the fact the man
was   carrying   food,   Diandre
questioned his presence.

"Diandre, he's obviously delivering
food."

"Quit being a smart ass and shut
your mouth."

Sensing danger, the delivery man
mustered up enough courage to voice
his opinion.

"Why don't you mind your business?
This doesn't have anything to do with
you."

"Leave the man alone, Diandre."

"Didn't I tell you to shut up?"

"Didn't I make it clear I don't give a
fuck what you said?"

Diandre was silent when he let me
go.   He appeared to have finally
calmed down. I straightened out my

clothes and waited for him to walk away. Instead, he scratched his head, looked at me, and hit me with a blow so hard to my face I felt dizzy. Though I could barely think straight, I managed to kick him in the groin. He yelled out in pain then hit me a second time causing me to black out.

When I came to, Lee was standing over the couch looking at me. I could see she'd been crying which made me break down. She explained she'd called the police while Diandre and I were talking. They'd escorted him away. Hearing the news only made the tears continue to flow. I was silent. I should have listened to my brother. Perhaps all of this could have been avoided. I asked Lee to call Donte, she already had. I already knew Donte would be furious. He was very over-protective and he'd be feeling like he failed to protect me. I was ready to hear all he had to say. Lee already had a heads up and informed me I hadn't heard the half of it.

Three knocks were heard on Lee's front door. She started for the door but I asked to answer it.

"It's Donte."

"How can you be so sure?"

"Trust me on this one."

I opened the door. Donte took one look at me and immediately pulled me into his arms. I really needed his strong embrace. He escorted me back into the living room to the couch. Lee closed the door. I didn't want to face my brother right now but I had to. I sat on the couch and held my throbbing head. Lee brought me an ice pack as Donte sat next to me.

My brother shook his head. I knew he was hurt. There was plenty he could say but he had a loss of words. My brother stared at my swollen face and dropped his head.

"Tell me everything."

"You're in danger."

"I pieced that much together, Donte."

"No, Dezzy it goes beyond the surface."

"I don't understand."

"Dezzy, Diandre is a sought after con artist who preys on women."

I was certain I hadn't heard my brother correctly. What he was claiming happened in the movies, not real life. I searched my brother's face to see if he was pulling my leg. His expression was very serious.

"I know this sounds bogus but I need you to hear me out."

"I'm listening."

"Diandre isn't Diandre at all. His name is Anthony Towers."

"Why haven't I heard the name before?"

"Because he constantly changes his identity. He goes under for several months at a time before surfacing again."

"If he's such a fugitive, why haven't-"

"He's known for coaxing young women into believing he is their knight in shining armor. He invests a lot of time and energy into the selected women causing them to fall in love. Once he's certain he's won a woman's heart he moves them away from their family. As she becomes distant with family and friends, she becomes more dependent and trusting of him... until..."

"Until what, Donte?"

"Until he kills them."

"What! Donte if they know he's guilty why is he still walking the streets?"

"Well-"

"Donte, there's no such thing as a black serial killer."

"Don't be so sure and quit cutting me off."

"Well, if he's a woman killer, explain his son's mother."

"Justine?"

"Yeah, how did you know?"

"Justine's name is Kimberly Watkins. She figured out who he was before he could harm her. Rather than turn him in, she joined his life of crime. Together, these sick bastards prey on innocent women for the hell of it."

"Donte, all of this brings me back to my original question. If the cops know all of this, why are they still walking the streets?"

"He's smart, Dezzy. He's found some sort of way to kill without getting his hands dirty."

MacGuyver and Nino Brown came to mind. A knot formed in the pit of my stomach and my mouth became dry. I asked Lee for a glass of water as my brother and I continued talking. I was full of questions and I was going to get as many answers from my brother as I could.

"Where does Kendrick fit into the picture?"

"Kendrick is as innocent as the next kid. They never wanted children but when she became pregnant they figured a way to incorporate him into their master plan."

"My God, how could I not recognize any of this before?"

"Dezzy, the man is a professional. You weren't supposed to figure it out."

I was struggling to accept the fact the man I loved wanted to kill me. I honestly believed the love he felt was sincere. I immediately began replaying various moments we spent together. When I gave serious thought, there were red flags – his jealousy after his party, references made to time spent with friends, and his sudden controlling temper.

"Dezzy, I want you to move back home until we can figure out what to do."

"I'm one step ahead of you. Lee thanks for the offer but I'm going to head home."

"No worries, girl... you just be careful and call me if I can do anything to help."

Donte walked me to my car. I waited for him to get in his car then he trailed me home. Once we got home, I hopped in his car so we could get something to eat – I never did satisfy my hunger. When we returned, Camille's BMW was parked in the driveway. Donte parked on the street. We were walking up to the house when Camille jumped out the car.

"Lee told me what happened. Oh my God, look at your face!"

"I'd rather not."

She followed me and Donte in the door. She spoke briefly to him but he knew it was nothing personal. I walked into the kitchen and sat at the table. Camille helped herself to a glass of apple juice and sat down with me. I focused on my food. I didn't want to look Camille in the eye because I knew she'd be devastated and I didn't want to begin crying all over again.

"What happened, D? Why didn't you tell me?"

"I'm having problems accepting this myself right now, Camille."

"Dezzy, I am so sorry."

"Don't be sorry, Camille. It's not your fault."

I told Camille everything Donte had told me. She was completely dumbfounded. She was going to relay all of this information to Blu but I begged her not to. I wasn't supposed to know any of this. If she mentioned this to Blu and he suddenly began acting differently,

Diandre would know something wasn't right.

Donte overheard our conversation and reinforced the importance of not mentioning anything to anyone. He also added I would already have hell on my hands once Kimberly received word he'd been arrested. Camille began moving around aimlessly – something she only did when she was nervous. She inquired about anything she could do to help. Donte recommended she stay strong for me and let justice be served by his father.

"Donte, what makes them so sure they'll catch him red handed?"

"Well for one, they've arrested one of the men he hires to do hits. If he talks, they'll have enough to bring him in and most likely get him."

"What if the man won't talk?"

"Well considering all the dirt he's done, he's going to try and get any deal he can. The cops will tell him what he wants to hear in order to get what they want. All they need is for him to testify in court."

"What if he gets to me before they have a chance?"

"That is not going to happen."

"How can you be so certain, D? They are going to let him go in a few hours if I don't press charges."

"Well, don't press charges right now, he'll walk. Besides, we don't want to make him any more upset. We want him to get caught on murder charges not domestic abuse."

I was hoping I would wake up and find myself in the middle of a bad dream. When I touched the right side of my face, everything became a reality – my swollen face was very real.

I dreaded having to tell my mother why I'd be moving back into her house. She believed I hadn't thought everything through in the first place. My returning to her home would prove her right. In addition, she would be furious and worry herself to death. I decided I wouldn't mention anything until she came back from her trip.

Camille stayed for another hour before returning home. She had no control over the situation and it bothered her. She assured me her cell phone would be on and she'd be taking all calls if I needed her. Donte walked her to her car and I went into my almost bare room. My bed and television were still here along with a few other belongings. I yearned for my bed. After the day from hell, I only wanted to sleep. I prayed I could sleep the pain away.

Chapter Twelve

Lee was a lifesaver. She'd managed to get the swelling around my eye to go down tremendously. Unfortunately, the skin was still black and blue. While I longed for my face to return to normal, I didn't panic because if push came to shove I was hoping my eye wasn't anything a little M.A.C makeup couldn't fix. Lee finished applying a cold ointment to my eye then sat down next to me on the couch. Camille was preparing a fire in the fireplace while Lee and I fingered through DVDs to watch. We decided on *Friday*. This movie was one that always lifted our spirits during depressing times. While Camille contained the fire, she briefly mentioned Diandre had stopped by her house. It was difficult for her to act as though nothing happened but she managed. He'd stopped by to discuss business with Blu but didn't leave before inquiring whether or not

Camille knew he'd hit me. He apologized repeatedly to her and swore he would never hit me again. He had her tell me because he was convinced I wouldn't hear him out – he was right.

We were forty five minutes into the movie when the doorbell rang. I didn't bother to pause the movie because I knew it like the back of my hand. I got up off of the couch and opened the front door. Considering the circumstances, I should've asked who was standing on the other side but I opened the door before I had a chance to give it a second thought. Diandre stood at the door with a single rose in his hand and the other behind his back. He wanted to talk about what had happened and apologize for what he'd done. I found myself becoming nervous. I wanted to move but my feet were cemented to the floor.

"Dezzy, can I speak with you?" He sounded like the Diandre I'd fallen in love with.

I couldn't speak if I wanted to. My entire body was immobile. I was looking at him and wanted to express so much. It was hard for me to even fathom the idea he was capable of murder but there was no denying the truth.

"Dezzy." He repeated my name with force but was careful not to overstep the boundary.

The tone of his voice frightened me, though, causing me to replay the day before in my mind. Suddenly, I felt lightheaded. Camille and Lee had placed the television on mute. They listened intently as they watched me at the door.

"Huh?" I asked in a daze.

"Are you all right?" He sounded genuinely concerned.

"No. I don't feel so good."

Lee stood up and walked over to me at the door. I was now holding on to the door for balance.

"What's wrong, Dezzy?" She asked.

I didn't answer the question. I clutched my stomach as I felt forced to bend over. I was light headed.

"I just want to lie down."

"Come on, Dezzy. I'll help you."

Lee began helping me back over to the couch. Diandre pleaded for my attention. Camille walked over to the door and suggested he try to call and speak with me – now wasn't a good time. Once Camille convinced him to leave, she came and joined me and Lee on the couch.

"He's gone now, Dezzy... you can relax."

"No... I really do feel sick... I... I ... I have to throw up!"

I stood up from the couch and made a bee-line to the bathroom. In a matter of moments, I was huddled over the toilet dry-heaving since I hadn't eaten anything. I hate throwing up but I'd much rather have something to throw up if it must happen. Lee came and stood in the doorway of the bathroom. She reminded me of my mother, the way she stood there with one hand on her hip. She watched me struggle for a moment before saying anything.

"When was the last time you had your period?"

"Huh? Oh please, Lee I'm just a little sick."

"Whatever... answer the question."

I'd never been good at keeping track of my periods. So long as my period came once a month, I didn't pay it much mind. While giving Lee's question thought, I realized it had been a while since I'd had one.

"Girl, I don't know."

"Oh boy, you know what this means, right?"

I was silent. I knew what Lee was insinuating but I didn't want to believe I was actually pregnant. If the circumstances were different, I may have actually been happy but knowing I could possibly be pregnant with Diandre's baby made my mood quickly revert to depression.

"I have a pregnancy test in my trunk, you can take it if you want to."

"I don't really have much choice... and why do you have a pregnancy test in your trunk?"

"Stay out of grown folks business."

"Whatever... can you bring it to me?"

Lee left me alone in the bathroom. I had the urge to cry but I fought it. If it turned out I was pregnant, it wasn't the end of the world. Of course, I wouldn't choose to be a single mother but if faced with the situation I could handle it. Camille informed me Donte was dropping Raijean off and would return shortly. Camille and Lee would remain by my side until he did. Lee handed me the test and walked out of the bathroom. I stared at the small box before finally opening it. I removed a small plastic cup and foil-wrapped applicator. All of my life I've looked forward to the day I'd take a pregnancy test and learn I was pregnant but today I was leery about the results.

I squatted over the toilet, cup in hand, and forced myself to use the bathroom. I walked out of the bathroom before anything could happen. I wanted to know but was afraid at the same time. When I came and sat back in the living room, both Lee and Camille were starring at me waiting on the results.

"I was too afraid to look."

"Girl! Do you want me to go in there and look for you?"

"Would you, Lee? I don't think I can."

Lee hopped up and walked into the bathroom. I sat motionless until she returned to the living room. I searched her face for answers but she revealed nothing. She sat next to me on the couch and looked at me. Camille, as if reading my mind, demanded the answer before I could part my lips.

"It's positive."

Lee's words echoed in my head. I was having a hard time accepting the truth. She placed her hand on my shoulder and gave a tight squeeze. Camille closed her eyes and lowered her head. We were all taking in the reality of the moment.

"No matter what you decide, you know I'll stand behind you either way." Lee spoke with certainty.

I knew she would have my back regardless. Camille nodded in agreement. I knew with the love and support of family and friends, this baby wouldn't have to want for anything.

"Well, I'm not going to tell anyone yet."

"What are you going to do?"

"I'm going to keep my baby. The baby didn't do anything wrong so why should she be punished? Babies are a blessing. The timing may be bad but I'm certain this is a blessing in disguise."

"She?" Camille asked.

"I've always wanted a little girl."

"You'll get one."

We all continued to sit in silence. Donte walked through the door and picked up on the awkward mood in the room immediately. I didn't want anyone to know about the pregnancy but there was no denying my brother of the opportunity. I expected him to hit the roof but he was civil. In fact, our viewpoints were similar – my baby deserved a chance at life. Of course, he despised Diandre but he would love the baby all the same.

"Maybe you should tell Diandre, D. If he knows you're carrying his baby his attitude may be different towards you."

"I may tell him but at the same time I don't want him to feel like he has permanent ties to me."

"That's true too... give it thought and be certain to play your cards right."

Since Donte was home, Lee and Camille decided to retire for the night. They'd spent the day with me, now it was time to go our separate ways. I appreciated their support more than words could ever express. We promised to touch bases with one another the next day then said our goodbyes. I ran up the stairs to my bedroom to grab my cordless phone and a blanket. Moments later, I returned to the living room and lied down by the fireplace. The entire room was silent with the exception of the popping in the fireplace. I laid on my back and envisioned my future. I had no control over what the future would bring but I could control the way I responded to the cards I was dealt. I intended to be the sole provider for my child. My mother had proven being a single mother would be trying but could be done. I planned to do the same.

As I stared at the ceiling, I began wondering if Diandre should know. He hadn't killed Justine, surely he couldn't kill me – I'm his child's mother too. Besides, Donte's father was a top notch detective. I believed he would make sure justice was served and spare my life in the process. In which case, I decided to tell Diandre. I wasn't sure what I'd gain from telling him, I only hoped he'd do the right thing.

I hadn't realized I'd dozed off until my phone rang and startled me awake. I answered on the second ring. Diandre spoke softly on the other end. Despite the urge to end the call immediately, I remained on the line. After all, he couldn't harm me through the phone and listening wouldn't hurt anything.

"Look, I fucked up and I know I did but baby, I'm sorry. I'm going to get help... please don't leave me."

"Diandre, I'm a woman not a punching bag. I can't believe you put your hands on me!"

"Dezzy, it's like I was watching myself from another point of view. I had no control."

To an extent, I believed him. Whenever he would have an episode he became another person. His eyes became vacant and he'd be overbearing and his overall demeanor was violent. Either way, my character never changed and I didn't deserve the cruel treatment. Despite his attempts, there was nothing Diandre could say that would convince me to take him back. I refused to be the same fool twice.

"Dezzy, I've apologized repeatedly. I don't know what more you want me to do."

"There's nothing you can do. You'll always have a special place in my heart but I'd be crazy to stay with you."

"Would you be willing to come back once I started counseling?"

Diandre's persistence was something I used to admire; now it was annoying. He was used to having his way but I refused to give in. Perhaps if I didn't know the circumstances surrounding his past, getting back together after he'd retrieved help was something I'd consider. After all, I really cared about Diandre and would have looked forward to spending the rest of our lives together. He'd been the knight in shining armor I always hoped for. Considering the conditions of the relationship now, though, the belief "if something is too good to be true, it probably is" proved itself to be more than evident.

"Diandre, how can you be so sure you'll change after counseling?"

"I gave you my word."

"You also said you'd never hit me but that fell through."

"Come home, baby. I will make it up to you."

"I'm not in the mood."

"You're not in the mood? You're always in the mood."

"Well not today... I'm going to refrain for a while."

"Why? Are you seeing someone else?"

"Of course not, I need time to clear my head and figure some things out."

"Okay, so you don't want to see me in person. Is there anything I can do over the phone?"

"I don't think so but if I change my mind I'll let you know."

"You used to include me on your thoughts and decision-making."

"So far Diandre, that hasn't changed but I need time to myself."

"All right, I'll respect that. Can I call you later?"

"That's fine. We'll talk later, goodbye."

I ended the call before he had a chance to get in another word. I was crying because I felt torn and helpless. I really wanted to believe everything was a huge misunderstanding but I knew better. I strived my entire life to avoid drama at all costs only to have it sneak up and bite me in the ass. I've been scarred and in nine months I'll have a constant reminder of my worst nightmare.

I was adding another log to the fire when Donte walked into the living room carrying his sleeping bag and Scrabble. He sat his things down as the doorbell rang. After letting in several gusts of cold wind, he returned with pizza. He popped a mixed CD into the stereo, set up the game then gestured for me to join him at the coffee table.

"Dezzy, it's been a while since we've had a night alone to kick back like we used to back in the day."

"I'll say... its unfortunate the shit had to hit the fan in order for this to happen, though."

"You know what, the way this came to be doesn't matter. What matters is we're alive, well, and fortunate to spend this time with one another so let's enjoy it – can't cry over spilled milk."

"We're only missing one thing to make this night complete."

"Mama won't be home for three more days."

"Having mama around would add a nice touch but that's not what I'm talking about."

He turned his attention from the game and looked at me. Our eyes communicated with each other but we said nothing. It didn't take long for my brother to catch my drift.

"The Simpsons," we said in unison.

Donte checked the time and declared all game play would cease in an hour – we had to watch The Simpsons. A chance to play and be carefree was what I needed; Donte never failed to have my back. He inhaled his fifth piece of pizza while I worked on my third. Between bites, we each created words and took turns rapping verses and singing hooks off of his disc of rap jams. Before long, The Simpsons had come and gone, the pizza was nonexistent and the stereo had blast its last song.

Rather than retire for the night, my brother and I remained in the living room and enjoyed one another's company until the sun began to rise. Although we're very close, I learned a lot about my brother that night and he the same. It was amazing how we'd both crept into adulthood and already began dealing with the trials and tribulations it entailed. Needless to say, neither of us had encountered a problem too much to bear – when and if we did, we'd always have one another to pull us through.

Chapter Thirteen

I woke with popcorn stuck to my cheek and my brother's foot in my face. He was too long for the couch so his feet were hanging over the arm rest. I had one mind to hit his foot and wake him up but judging by the way he was calling hogs, I decided to let him sleep. I pulled myself off of the floor and began cleaning up around him. Since I'd be braiding hair today, I'd arranged for my clients to come to my home rather than go into the shop. The skin around my eye was still bruised and I didn't want the other females I worked with asking questions. I'd managed to keep the majority of my private life to myself and I intended to keep everything the same.

My bubble bath wasn't as long as usual but it served its purpose. After a night of sleeping on the floor, my bones and muscles ached – the hot water was what my body needed.

I threw on a baby blue cotton sweat suit and slippers. I had a full day ahead and I wanted to be as comfortable as possible. While combing my hair, I began to feel nauseous but managed to hold myself together. I prayed my entire pregnancy wouldn't be this way. If so, this was going to be the longest nine months of my life!

As I headed back down the stairs to grab a bite to eat before my first client, Donte staggered past me mumbling words that suggested his bed would do him far better than the couch. He also explained he'd only have an hour more of sleep before leaving to take Raijean for a check up.

I had a boiled egg and a piece of toast. By the time I'd finished my glass of apple juice, the doorbell rang. I put my glass in the sink and went to open the door for my client. All of my clients knew to come prepared since I didn't have the convenience of a wash bowl at home. Not to mention, the time would be cut down. After we confirmed the hairstyle of choice, I began braiding.

I was halfway into my second client's hair when my doorbell rang, again. Assuming it was my final client of the day, I opened the door. Diandre stood at the door holding a bouquet of flowers in one hand while waving a white cloth in the other. I wanted to slam the door in his face for taking it upon himself to come to my home without asking or calling but I didn't want to cause a scene. My third client walked up behind him – they both came inside.

Observing the looks on my clients' faces, they were curious to know who Diandre was. He'd only come to the shop a few times and when he did it was late so most of my clients never saw him. Under normal conditions, I would've introduced him to everyone but I no longer felt it necessary. He walked up to me, brushed the hair back that was covering my eye and kissed my cheek. If they didn't know who he was, I'm sure they had an idea now. I cringed on the inside but managed to hold my composure. I continued to braid hair while my other client placed my flowers in a vase.

Diandre had taken the liberty in seating himself on the couch as my brother came down the stairs. He saw Diandre and began walking in our direction. Preparing for the worst, I asked my client to join the other in the kitchen. I informed her to help herself to some food while I concluded some unfinished business. Once my client was in the kitchen and out of earshot, I turned my attention back to the two men in the living room.

"Nigga, you must be crazy or extremely bold." Donte said.

"Come again?"

"You know what the fuck I'm talking about. I didn't like your ass from day one. What in the hell made you think you could put your hands on my sister?"

"Dawg, you're in some business that doesn't concern you."

"It became my business when you blacked her eye."

"I don't owe you an explanation."

"What?"

Donte began walking towards Diandre who was now standing. I stepped between the two of them. Donte tried to push past me but I refused to let him by. He was not thinking rationally so someone had to. He had been the main one telling me to stay cautious and calm but had become the first one to jump bad. I feared my brother was only making matters worse. I had to think fast.

"Look, both of you need to calm down. I am working here and all of this is far from professional."

"You need to check your brother, Dezzy."

"Diandre, I can deal with my brother later. Right now, I need you to either take your seat so we can talk or leave."

He studied Donte hard then took his seat. My brother didn't want to leave me alone with him but I believed I would be safe, especially since he was already walking on thin ice. He assured me he and Raijean would be back and not to hesitate to call should I need him. He walked to the door and shut it slowly behind him.

"Why are you telling our business?"

"Diandre, I didn't have to say anything. My brother took one look at my eye and knew I didn't do this to myself."

"Who else knows?"

"Diandre, why are you here?"

"Well, I hoped I'd come and we'd reconcile our relationship."

"What for, Diandre? What good is a relationship without trust?"

"I agree but we can start over. There is no need to dwell in the past. Now is as good a time as any to have a new beginning."

"True and maybe a new beginning would mean us going our separate ways."

"So much for a future together, huh?"

"You should have thought about a future before you jeopardized it."

I was trying to find the right time to tell him about the baby. He seemed open and willing to communicate. I hoped his attitude would change once he knew. I had clients to attend to so I couldn't procrastinate much longer. I needed to get it over with and deal with what was to follow.

"Diandre, I need to tell you something."

"I'm listening."

"Do you remember how I suddenly felt sick yesterday?"

"Yeah... I knew you were mad but you didn't have to—"

"I'm not finished."

"I'm sorry... continue."

"I threw up."

I was having a hard time communicating my thoughts with words. Diandre could tell I was avoiding something but he didn't press the issue.

"I'm going to the doctor tomorrow because I haven't had a period in a while."

He removed his hands from his pockets and sat on the edge of the couch. He knew what I was trying to say but he didn't mutter a word. Instead, he watched me and waited for the conclusion of this drawn out explanation I was giving.

"Diandre, I'm pregnant."

"Are you sure?"

"I took a test and it was positive."

"Have you already decided what you are going to do?"

"I don't believe in abortions."

His facial expression didn't reveal how he felt about my decision. I expected him to be somewhat delighted. He lowered his head and remained quiet for five minutes. When he did speak, he announced his departure. He leaned towards me to get a kiss but I backed away. He didn't press the issue. Instead, he silently walked past me and out the door. I went into the kitchen to get my clients and complete the task I'd started. I wasn't sure what to think about Diandre's reaction but I decided I wouldn't rack my brain trying to figure it out.

After I walked my last client to the door, I retreated to my room in order to relax. I wasn't in the mood to mingle so I let Donte and Raijean have time to themselves in the living room. My brother had picked up pamphlets about pregnancy and breast-feeding while waiting for Raijean when they were at the doctor so I would evaluate them in the privacy of my bedroom.

I enjoyed a hot shower while listening to Anita Baker. I knew how to hold a tune but I sounded especially decent in the shower. Once I'd finished, I burned incents and candles around my room then sprawled out across my bed to air dry. I'd finished reviewing my second pamphlet when my phone rang.

"How's everything going, mommy?"

"Hey, Lee... how're you?"

"Fine now that I'm not dealing with those patients. How are you?"

"Decent... I told him."

"What happened?"

"He didn't really say anything. He stood up and left."

"Left... he was there?"

"That's a whole different story."

Judging by my tone, Lee didn't bother to question me further. She remained silent and allowed me to communicate my feelings on my own time. At the end of my speech, I began bawling. I'd never felt so alone in my life. Granted, I had friends and family who would do everything in their power to assist me, it wasn't their responsibility. Any chance of reconciliation with Diandre was nonexistent as far as I was concerned. If he wasn't going to be there for me now when I needed him most, I knew I couldn't depend on him for anything else. Lee consoled me to the best of her ability but there was nothing anyone could say to soothe the way I was feeling. It's amazing how one can think they know someone only to learn they know nothing at all. As I've always believed, people can't be given too much credit because they never cease to fail one another.

"D, as much as you'd like to have Diandre in your child's life, you can do it on your own."

"I know I can and I will. I don't want to do it alone, though."

"As long as I continue to breathe you'll never be alone and you know too many people. Between all of us, Diandre's shoes will be filled and then some. Don't sweat the dumb shit, Dezzy. You're time and energy is much too valuable and can be put into other things."

Lee always did know how to motivate me. My tears soon went away and I began feeling much more sure of myself. We conversed about other events happening in our lives when her doorbell rang.

"Dezzy, girl I have to go. I'll pick you up at nine for your appointment."

"Who's at your house?"

"Girl, I'm grown. I taught you what you know!"

"Whatever! I'll see you tomorrow."

I hung up the phone feeling as though I didn't have a care in the world. With new found energy, I got up and put on a pair of pajamas. Sitting around feeling sorry for myself wasn't going to change a damn thing. I picked up a notepad and began writing down items my baby would need. I would begin looking now and grabbing items as I came across them in order to maintain my sanity later.

After I'd made a thorough list, I slid it into my purse. I blew out the candles, opened the windows and turned out the lights. Occasionally, I had the opportunity to enjoy a clear midnight blue, moonlit sky from my bedroom window – this night was perfect. I sat in the window seal and peered out the window. I normally would sit and look out the window for hours on end but after posting myself in the window an awkward, eerie feeling came over me. When I looked down below, a car was in the middle of the street without headlights. Fortunately, my lights weren't on so I hid myself in the shadows as I continued to watch. Coming from the opposite direction was Diandre's Mercedes. He pulled next to the car and held conversation. Gestures were made towards my house as I remained frozen. I couldn't make out the person behind the wheel of the car facing my direction. When Diandre handed an envelope through his window to the other car, Justine's face came into clear view as she received it. A knot formed in the pit of my stomach as my mind began to run wild. Diandre continued up the street to the stop sign then made a left – he was no longer in my sight. Justine coasted past my house then turned off in another direction.

I wanted to believe I hadn't seen Diandre and his accomplice casing my house but I knew my eyes hadn't failed me. My suspicions were confirmed when my telephone began ringing across the bedroom – Diandre's number appeared on the caller id. I decided I wasn't going to answer it. Instead, I jumped up and threw clothes and toiletries in an overnight bag. I snatched off my pajamas and threw on a pair of jeans and a sweat shirt. I was down the stairs and informing Donte of everything I'd saw in a spilt second. My brother and Raijean wasted no time getting dressed and grabbing the bare necessities. Between the three of us, we secured the house, set the alarm and headed for a hotel until we had an opportunity to contact Donte's father.

At this point, I wasn't sure where we were headed and I didn't want to know. I left a message for Lee to cancel the doctor's appointment and didn't mention anything more. The less everyone knew the better. I sat in complete silence and said silent prayers until we finally reached our destination. My brother got us a room at the Hilton near the Oakland Airport under an assumed name. Granted, I was aware Diandre had an undisclosed past and was capable of more than I could ever fathom, I hadn't accepted the fact my life was in jeopardy until now. My mother always said God wouldn't give me any more than I could handle. Now, I only prayed He'd have mercy.

Chapter Fourteen

Donte left Raijean and me in the hotel room while he'd gone out to meet up with his father. He'd called thirty minutes ago to inform us he and his father would return shortly. In the meantime, Raijean and I had breakfast in the room. She put a dent in her food while I poked at mine with a fork. I knew I needed to eat something but my nerves had me on edge. Although I wasn't paying attention to the program on the television, I pretended to be engrossed. Donte had forgiven Raijean but I was still having a hard time. I didn't want her trying to bond with me. I know my attitude may not be the best to have but she had really taken my brother through unnecessary drama and whether she intended to or not, I went through it too.

The phone sitting next to Raijean began to ring. Before the ring could be completed, she'd answered the phone. Her expression immediately turned to one of panic. She sat motionless while listening to the other end. Before I had a chance to question who was speaking to her, she handed me the phone.

"Why are you running from me?"

"How did you find where I was?"

"Haven't you figured out by now I have pull everywhere I go?" His tone was cocky and conniving.

"Look, Diandre I thought I made it clear I no longer want to have a relationship with you. Why don't you make your point or I am going to hang up the phone."

"I wouldn't do that if I were you."

"What's that supposed to mean?"

"You're clever, figure it out."

That was it. I was tired of being on edge. This man had caused me to completely shut down and become another person. I hadn't led a normal life in what felt like an eternity. I decided whatever happened was destined – I wasn't going to run any longer. I refused to walk on eggshells the rest of my life. It was time to face the music and I believed I would survive.

"I don't doubt my intelligence. Be a man and leave no room for confusion."

"Oh, is little Dezzy trying to step to me?"

"I'm trying to be an adult about this. Either you're going to cooperate or I am going to end this call."

For the first time, Diandre knew I was serious. He was silent on his end of the line. I imagined he was trying to come up with something sarcastic or ingenious to say. I stood up and was about to walk over to the nightstand to hang up the phone.

"You really don't know who you're dealing with."

"I think I have an idea."

"I'm capable of many things."

My body was beginning to fill with so much anger, I started trembling. I knew there was only a small matter of time before the police caught up with Diandre so I decided to raise the stakes a little. I intended to get even for all the hell I'd been through.

"I want you to know I don't expect you to do anything for my baby. There's no need for you to come around."

"Dezzy, you probably haven't given thought to this baby."

"Oh, I've given more thought than you know. In fact, I've come up with a few names... If it's a girl, Kimberly... If it's a boy, Anthony."

The silence on the other end of the line was so extreme, a rat could be heard pissing on cotton. Seconds later, I was greeted by a dial tone. It didn't matter. I knew I'd gotten to him. For the first time in a while, I felt as though I had peace within myself.

I was hanging up the phone when Donte and his father walked through the hotel door. They hadn't closed the door behind them before Raijean and I began blurting out what had taken place. Donte feared I may have acted too soon when Mr. Sutter gave the news we'd all been waiting on. The other hit man had been captured and both were talking. They'd already agreed to testify in court and were placed in protective custody in the meantime. Donte's father explained a warrant for Diandre's arrest would be available before the day ended. As soon as he had the warrant in his hand, he'd pay the conniving bastard a visit. Once Diandre was in custody, Justine would be soon to follow.

I was so ecstatic, I felt like I was floating. All of the pieces of the puzzle were finally falling into place. I couldn't wait to sit in the courtroom and watch justice be served. Diandre had finally messed with the wrong woman and now he and his crew were going to pay. His dark past had finally caught up with him.

Normally, I would dread leaving a hotel room like this one but I was eager to return home. Though there wasn't much to return to in terms of my material belongings, I looked forward to starting over. Everything that was at Diandre's house would remain there – that was now the past and I wasn't looking back. It was time to move on, once again, and get my life together. I was going to undergo some serious changes in the future and this time I would make sure I was ready.

Mr. Sutter remained at the house with me and Donte until he received the call confirming the warrant. He immediately began making phone calls to initiate action. He shared comforting words with me, shook his son's hand, and walked out the front door.

"See Dezzy, no worries. Everything is going to be fine. Mama will be back tomorrow and she doesn't have to know any of this ever happened."

"Unless I decide to tell her... What should I do with the ring?"

"Get your coat. I know a place where you can get the value of the ring and then some. You can put the money towards my nephew's college fund."

"Yeah, I'm sure your niece will appreciate it."

"Whatever!" Donte playfully shoved me out the front door. Moments later, we were headed to an underground location.

Blood is thicker than water. Donte never ceased to amaze me with the way he stayed dedicated to his family. There was nothing or no one who could ever break the bond my mother, brother, and I shared. I realized I was fortunate so I promised myself I would never associate with anyone who threatened that bond again. This was one promise I intended to keep.

I let Donte do all of the talking inside of the pawn shop. It's unfortunate, but there is an unspoken respect men automatically received over women. Since I knew this to be true, I allowed my brother to get the better deal. When the agent realized Donte wasn't going to back down, he surrendered. I politely collected the cash then Donte and I headed to the bank to open a savings account. The money was for the baby and if it weren't easily accessible it would be much harder to pinch off of.

In light of the moment, my brother and I decided to celebrate. He treated me to lunch at Baker's Square in San Lorenzo then we headed to Bay Fair Mall. He and I both put a hurting on our wallets purchasing clothes for both of our unborn children. Once the bags became too many to carry, we retired for the evening. We returned home and would remain there until we received the call with the good news.

I was dusting all of the picture frames while my brother fluffed the pillows on the couch. My mother was a neat freak and her home was to be in order when she returned. Donte was going to begin the bathrooms when a melodic knock began on the front door. My brother immediately stopped what he was doing and ran to the front door. On the other side, stood his childhood friend Khalil who left to join The Navy several years ago.

"D!"

"Oh snap! What's up, Khalil? What are you doing here?"

"Can't a brother return home every once and a while?"

"Of course! How long will you be here?"

"I'm here for good."

"You're done! Khalil, it's about to be on and cracking!"

"Dawg, can I come in?" He laughed.

"Oh, my fault. Come on in. You remember Dezzy, right?"

"Damn, Dezzy the last time I saw you, you were far from grown."

"How're you doing, Khalil? It has been a long time."

Time in the service had done Khalil very well. He was my first crush but I'd never told him. If he was anything like he was when we were younger, he would be the ideal man. Any woman fortunate enough to have him should count her blessings. Within five seconds, I'd already scoped Khalil from head to toe. There was no ring to indicate him as off limits. The urge to flirt was there but I dismissed it. I needed time to myself to heal. A man on the rebound wouldn't be good for either party involved.

Donte and Khalil took a seat on the couch and began catching up with one another on all of the lost time. Fearing the house wouldn't be in order before my mother returned, I continued to clean. I took occasional pauses to comment on different subject matters they were discussing when Donte asked but otherwise I minded my own business. Once I'd finished cleaning, I joined the guys in the living room. No sooner than I'd sat down, Donte stood and headed to the kitchen to put a frozen pizza in the oven.

"So how are you, Dezzy? I know you have a lot going on right now. Are you all right?"

"I'll be much better once I receive the call from Mr. Sutter."

"I know that's right. Other than that, what's going on with you?

Women's intuition had never failed me before and if my instincts served me correctly, Khalil was flirting with me. "What do you mean?"

"I mean... would you be open to mingling with an old friend?"

"On a date... with you?"

"Don't sound so shocked and is that so hard to believe?"

"No, not at all. Are you sure you'd want to? I mean, I'm not certain I'd make the best company for you right now."

"I can judge for myself. What do you say?"

"I guess I'm available."

"Is tomorrow night for dinner okay?"

"That'll be fine."

Donte rejoined us in the living room. We talked and enjoyed one another's company until the pizza was ready. I had one slice and allowed the two of them to devour the rest. While they ate, I headed upstairs to have a long, steamy shower. I'd bonded enough; it was time to do my own thing.

I picked out my clothing for the week and gave my room a thorough cleaning. Once I'd finished, I made calls to all of my clients who were booked for the next day informing them to return to the shop. I blew the dust off of my journal and began pouring my heart out onto the pages. It had been a while since I had done writing of this kind but it was my second nature. When I felt I didn't have anything more to say, I put on flannel pajamas and my house shoes then returned downstairs.

Donte and Khalil were wearing gym shorts and t-shirts. Khalil spun a basketball on one finger while Donte laced up his tennis shoes. He double-knotted the laces then jumped up from the couch. Donte hadn't noticed I'd rejoined them in the living room. Khalil sat the basketball down and acknowledged me.

"Hey, Dezzy we're going to go shoot some hoops up the street."

"D, we'll only be gone for a couple of hours. Put the alarm on and stay by the phone. My father should be calling any minute."

"I'll be fine. You guys have fun. Donte, don't forget your key."

"It's in my bag. Lock the door behind us, okay?"

"Yes, Donte."

I locked the door behind them then took a seat on the couch. I picked up the remote control for the television when I remembered I needed to set the alarm. As I headed for the kitchen, the phone began to ring as three knocks banged on the door simultaneously. I figured I'd have enough time to let Donte in and catch the phone. I jogged over to the door and answered it without hesitation.

"What did you forget?"

I was prepared to give my brother a hard time. Instead, I stared down the barrel of a gun. The machine had already answered the call. Donte's father sounded distraught as he explained Diandre received a tip and had escaped before they could capture him.

"Hi, bitch." Justine stated. "If you scream I won't hesitate to pull the trigger."

She cocked the gun then pushed past me into the house. She headed over to the coffee table and dropped a manila envelope. She headed back in my direction but turned away and walked towards the answering machine. She played the message once again then erased it. I wanted to run but I was certain I had nowhere to go. She walked up to me, pressed the gun into my back and forced me out of my house.

"Don't try to be a hero or I'll cancel your ass."

I cooperated with her and walked over to a rusty brown Nissan Sentra. She forced me into the backseat and slammed the door shut behind me. Once inside, I noticed there were no door handles. Diandre was sitting behind the wheel. He turned around and looked at me in disgust while Justine got into the car. She hadn't closed the door good behind her before he sped away from the house. Once we reached the corner, Diandre instructed me to blindfold myself with the bandana sitting next to me then handcuff myself. I did as I was told. We rode in silence for what felt like decades. I tried to rely on the swaying of my body for a sense of direction but it was pointless. Diandre was clever and was going out of his way to make sure I had no idea what was going on.

When the car finally came to a stop, I began to tremble. As much as I wanted to conceal my fear, it was impossible. Two car doors slammed shut then there was silence. I didn't know what to expect so I remained frozen in fear. Seconds later, the back door opened and Diandre's strong grip yanked me out. He pinned me against the car as he removed the handcuffs and blindfold. It took a few seconds for my eyes to readjust but no time to realize we were back at his cabin – in the middle of nowhere! Justine stood in the doorway of the cabin as Diandre pushed me over.

Once inside the cabin, all of the furniture had been removed from the living room with the exception of one wooden chair which Diandre forced me into. Justine headed over to assist him in tying me to the chair. When they were finished, the only movement I was capable of was breathing.

"So, did you miss me baby?"

I pierced Diandre's eyes with mine. There was no mistaking the hate in my heart I felt for him. I didn't mutter a word. "You hear me talking to you. Open your fucking mouth!"

My eyes left Diandre long enough to notice Justine. She leaned against the wall, arms folded, appearing very nonchalant. She seemed the least bit fazed by what was taking place. She looked on with gratification. I could forget her having a change of heart and helping me in this time of need.

Diandre had begun yelling since I failed to acknowledge him. When he realized yelling wouldn't bring a reaction out of me either, he began slapping me repeatedly. Justine walked over and handed him a cellular phone. He paused from the beating to acknowledge her. Blood was pouring out the corner of my mouth. I wasn't sure what they were up to. I only prayed it didn't get any worse than this. Tears streamed down my face as Diandre informed me he was calling my brother. He dialed the number then placed the phone to my ear.

"Dezzy?" Donte asked. I hadn't heard the phone ring.

"Yeah." I said, sniffling. There was blood running from my nose.

From the sound of Donte's voice, he had been crying. His crying tore me up on the inside. I could hear Khalil yelling obscenities and threatening Diandre in the background.

"Tell your brother to look in the envelope." Diandre said. "I want his punk ass to be here when you die."

Donte informed me he knew and had given his father the address – the police were already on their way. Now, Donte would be in route too. The only reason he hadn't left was on the suggestion of his father who said I may call. I prayed someone would get here before Diandre turned deadly. Diandre snatched the phone before I could say anything further.

"Nigga, you better not touch my sister!" I could hear Donte yelling.

"Fuck you." Diandre replied then hung up.

Diandre handed the phone back to Justine who returned to her position on the wall.

"Now what?" she asked.

"We wait. In the meantime, Dezzy... why don't you and I have a small talk?"

He gently moved a piece of hair from my face. I tried to dodge his hand the best way I could but I was unsuccessful. Diandre noticed my attempts and pushed my head back into the chair. I was terrified but if I was going to die, there were some things I needed to know.

"Diandre, was everything a lie?"

"Yep."

"You never cared about me, did you?"

"At one point I did." Justine rolled her eyes in disgust.

"Diandre, why are you doing this to me? I am carrying your child." Justine looked surprised – the first emotion of the evening.

"I don't care about your baby. Besides, you didn't want me around anyway."

"Diandre, this is your child."

"Out of sight, out of mind."

I could tell any chance of me getting him to change his mind passed. I decided to remain silent because I didn't want to say anything to set him off further. I could hear police sirens in the distance growing near. If I could stall him a little while longer, everything would be okay.

"I told him no police in the letter!" Justine yelled.

"You're brother fucked things up, Dezzy!" He said.

Justine panicked and ran out the back door. Diandre seemed shocked at her reaction. Needless to say, he wasn't pleased at all. For the first time, he appeared nervous. This was unusual because Diandre always remained in control of everything.

"Well, Dezzy this is goodbye."

"It doesn't have to be, Diandre."

"Shut up!"

I did as I was told. I was saying silent prayers within. I wanted the police to hurry. I could see the lights outside the window. Moments later, I heard footsteps coming up to the door. Diandre cocked the trigger.

"Please don't do this, Diandre."

He looked me straight in the eyes.

"I never loved you!" He yelled, and then fired three shots.

I heard the police break down the door. Several of them wrestled Diandre to the ground while Mr. Sutter ran to my side.

"No, Dezzy... don't die on me baby.... I need an ambulance, now! Someone, please!"

I could hear an officer yelling to the others the female accomplice had been apprehended. Mr. Sutter untied me from the chair as Donte rushed through the door and over to my side. He attempted to lift me from the floor. I could feel his tears falling onto my face. I opened my mouth to speak but nothing came out. I was in excruciating pain but I was determined to speak.

"Donte, tell mama not to blame herself for this and that I love her. I love you too. Take care of her and promise me you're going to be okay."

"Dezzy, hang in there," he said between sobs. "You're going to be okay. You can tell her yourself."

I shook my head at my brother and forced a smile. A numbness came over my entire body then everything went black. It was all over now. I didn't have to worry. Diandre and Justine had been captured and they'd never harm anyone again. I only wished I'd lived to see it.

I had fallen in love with Diandre as my brother said I would. He meant everything to me and it was all a lie. In my encounters with men, love proved itself scandalous. I never understood why my luck couldn't be better. Now, I'd never know.

Qiana London

About the Author

Truly gifted, Qiana London takes her readers by storm with this urban, romance-thriller. An accomplished poet and playwright, she raises the bar for herself once again with the release of her first novel, *Scandalous Love*. Never before has she written with such force while addressing the taboo realities of life. A native of Oakland, Ca and recent graduate of the University of Southern California, Qiana London reinvents old-fashioned "story-telling". She resides in Hayward and Los Angeles, Ca.